GURKHA

The True Story of a Campaign for Justice

Peter Carroll

with a foreword by Joanna Lumley

GURKHA

The True Story of a Campaign for Justice

First published in Great Britain in 2012 by
Biteback Publishing Ltd
Westminster Tower
3 Albert Embankment
London
SE1 7SP
Copyright © Peter Carroll 2012

Peter Carroll has asserted his right under the Copyright, Designs and Patents
Act 1988 to be identified as the author of this work.

ISBN 978-1-84954-137-4

10 9 8 7 6 5 4 3 2 1

A CIP catalogue record for this book is available from the British Library.

Set in Chronicle and Grotesque by Namkwan Cho
Cover design by Namkwan Cho

Printed and bound in Great Britain by CPI Group (UK) Ltd, Croydon CR0 4YY

To Lynne, always and forever.

CONTENTS

———•❖•———

Foreword by Joanna Lumley   ix

Preface   xiii

One: First Faltering Steps   1

Two: Liverpool and Bournemouth   17

Three: First Breakthrough, Setbacks and Turmoil   26

Four: The Middle Years   35

Five: Fame   59

Six: High Court Start Day 17/9/2008   67

Seven: High Court End Day 30/9/2008   77

Eight: Black Friday   91

Nine: Parliament to the Rescue 100

Ten: Plotting 106

Eleven: The Commons Vote 113

Twelve: Joanna meets Mr Brown
6/5/2009 124

Thirteen: Phil Woolas 7/5/2009 129

Fourteen: Tears and Fish 'n' Chips
20/5/2009 141

Fifteen: Downing Street 21/5/2009 151

Sixteen: Nepal 25/7/2009 165

Seventeen: Dripping Toxin 224

Eighteen: And Still It Drips 238

Nineteen: Joanna, Daughter of Nepal
and Goddess of the Gurkhas 246

Twenty: Looking Back 262

Acknowledgements 266

FOREWORD

by Joanna Lumley

———•———

I received a message from my agent saying that a man called Peter Carroll was trying to get in touch with me about the Gurkhas; could I help? So strange: such a brief request; so ... well, so out of the blue.

I telephoned him and suddenly my life changed in a way that I could never have envisaged. For the next year the Gurkha Justice campaign took over my life, and although I was working on a thousand different projects in my professional career the campaign immediately became the most important commitment by far.

To my shame I, like many others, hadn't known that retired Gurkhas were treated differently from other veterans simply because Nepal has never been part of the Commonwealth. Their legendary courage and prowess in warfare was well known, and countless stories of their lethal skills combined with terrific humour have been retold by generations of soldiers. No one thought to question how they were treated when their soldiering days were done. I am the daughter of a Gurkha officer and spent all my young life following the flag and his regiment in India and the Far East. When the campaign started my father was no longer alive, nor was my mother, but I am sure they, like the rest of the armed forces, and the whole country, and the whole world, would have been outraged by the injustice, the sheer unfairness, of the fact that Gurkhas were not allowed to settle and work in the country they had defended so willingly for nearly 200 years. How didn't we know? Well, we didn't, and a great wrong had to be put right. Sleeves rolled up: what could I do to help?

The campaign was well under way by the time I met Peter and the lawyers of Howe and Co.; the press were mildly interested in the High Court test cases brought by four retired Gurkhas and a Gurkha widow with the help of the Legal Aid lawyers, but the campaign needed the oxygen of publicity to catch fire. In this excellent account of what actually happened you will read of our extraordinary journey, our meetings in doorways and cafés, our encounters in the corridors of power, our near despair and jubilation as the switchback ride of our search for justice began to rattle and roar through the land. Along the way those of us at the centre of the tornado became fast friends, and many a night was spent emailing each other after midnight with strategies and new contacts and proposals. All of us were working in the daytime on our 'day jobs' and apart from a colossally generous private donation to set up our website, we all picked up all the tabs.

There were five of us at the epicentre, which was contained within a closely supportive group, wrapped around us and buttressed by goodwill and optimism. People everywhere and from all walks of life were there when we most needed them; but as we approached the castle gates, as it were, the winds howled around us and victory seemed far away, if not actually impossible. I would not have missed one day of it – and to have been of service to these quite extraordinarily brave and constant friends, the indomitable hill men of Nepal, has made me immeasurably proud and happy. We can never repay them for the sacrifices they have made for our country, but fighting for them when they needed us has been a reward for me that I will treasure as long as I live.

We simply could not have succeeded as we did with the Gurkha Justice campaign were it not for Peter Carroll. His was the driving energy powering us through the months when the days were their darkest. His was the voice of reason that attracted the serious members of the fourth estate and got us column inches and brilliantly attended press conferences. His were the blueprints for many of the letters written and articles printed. His was the staying power to the very end and the voice that alerted me in the beginning, inviting me to join the campaign. I have worked with the press for over forty years and I have never met anyone who matched his innate skill for sensing when a story would break or when a strategy would go stale. He loves the press and, I think, is loved by them because he delivers the goods. My respect for his ability cannot be measured and my affection for him will never diminish. At the heart of this man is integrity, determination, courage, kindness and, when needed, a formidable measure of fire. He is the best: the very best.

Joanna Lumley

PREFACE

———•———

This book tells the compelling story of the Gurkha Justice campaign.

It was a campaign that stirred and united a nation, starting from humble and stumbling origins to be *the* campaign sensation of recent years. It put right a historical wrong. It brought honour back to our politics. It gave justice to some of our truest friends. It was a campaign that in turn shattered and made political reputations. It was at times heartbreaking and at others hysterically funny.

This is a story that justifies faith in human nature – an extraordinary account of how a lowly local politician more used to dealing with potholes in the streets of Kent, a firm of dedicated lawyers and a much loved actress overturned the policy of Her Majesty's

Government in spectacular style. Together, Joanna Lumley, the lawyers of Howe & Co. and I were fused into a whirlwind of a campaigning force that swept into the very heart of Downing Street and Westminster.

Few will realise just how small the group was and how loosely associated were the key players in the campaign. Many media commentators marvelled at the speed and dynamism of the campaign, often reporting it as 'slick and well oiled'. In reality, the campaign was almost comically under-resourced: the planning (such as it was) was carried out usually in the dead of night by emails flying between us; most 'formal' meetings took place in the coffee shop of the Jewel Tower opposite the House of Commons. That said, our unlikely alliance seemed to become greater than the sum of its parts and together we orchestrated a campaign envied by many for its verve, direction and power. We worked together, cried together, laughed together, cheered together and sometimes just sat in silence as we pondered the events that we had helped unleash.

We planned, we demonstrated, we marched, we petitioned, we lobbied. Our case was heard in the courts, in the Commons and in meetings with officials and Ministers – at least one over fish and chips ... and champagne.

The humour that somehow attaches itself to situations where ordinary people are doing extraordinary things runs like a golden thread through this story. I'm sure you'll smile when I tell you that I suggested to Joanna that she should challenge the government's failure to offer a meeting with the Prime Minister, as asked for in numerous letters, by simply phoning 10 Downing Street and requesting one – only for her to respond: 'But darling, I'm cleaning the oven in my marigolds.'

The incredible bond between so many in Britain and the brave hill soldiers of Nepal shone through during the entire campaign. There was a truly overwhelming response from people all around the world who wrote in with signatures of support and letters with personal accounts of how the Gurkhas had saved loved ones or inspired undying admiration.

The vast majority of Gurkha heroes had been treated shabbily by successive governments. Their lawyers at Howe & Co. led the legal charge against the government. These men of law had such an emotional bond with their clients that, on occasions, one partner could not speak of them without spontaneous tears.

And when we finally made the long and emotional journey to Nepal – a trip that started off with just four people then exploded into a virtual state visit with a full media entourage – the immense emotional response from the Gurkhas and their families in Nepal, the depth of love and affection shown, was incredible.

This whole experience has reaffirmed my belief that when good-minded people do good things – good things happen as a result. For anyone disillusioned or jaded by life, this book shows that the incredible can be achieved. For those who feel that democracy and politics can't deliver, this is at least one shining example of our country and its institutions at its best.

ONE

FIRST FALTERING STEPS

———•———

'Some people say that a small group of committed citizens can change the world ... in reality that's all that ever does change the world.' Margaret Mead

I suppose that all quotes become quotes because people see something profound in them, otherwise they'd just be a collection of words. For me, the quote above is not just true; it is fascinatingly true and is therefore in the Premier League of quotes. It's just so piercing in its summary of how we live and how all politics and great movements get going. Think about the abolition of slavery, anti-apartheid, workers' rights, suffrage ... all these world-changing movements started somewhere, either with an individual or a small group. We live in a world where it's easy to forget this.

We think that all our great institutions – our political parties, charities and campaign groups – have always just been there. They haven't. Somebody, somewhere, at some point in time had the burning desire to change something. It would be their efforts, almost always with the help of only a very few, that would generate the whole movement. Macmillan Cancer Support, for example, one of the UK's leading charities, was started by just one man, Douglas Macmillan, in 1911. So it is with nearly every movement for social change.

As what became known as the Gurkha Justice campaign grew from its humble beginnings into a national campaign, overturning the policy of Her Majesty's Government, Margaret Mead's words continued to grow on me. Now I think that quote sums up the spirit of what we did exactly. Initially we were a very small group of people, and yet for thousands of retired Gurkha heroes what we started changed the world.

I had moved to Folkestone in 2000 to start the long process of campaigning there as the Liberal Democrat prospective parliamentary candidate for the constituency of Folkestone & Hythe. The incumbent MP was the Rt Hon. Michael Howard MP. After a very prominent career, he was now on the back benches and seen to be potentially vulnerable to 'tactical' voting. For those not au fait with the jargon of politics, tactical voting is where people decide on how to vote based on how best their vote can be used to beat the candidate least desirable in their eyes. Though a remarkably able and successful politician in his time, the electoral results for Folkestone & Hythe did suggest that if enough people in his constituency who would normally be classed as Labour voters could instead be persuaded to vote Liberal Democrat, then Michael Howard might be toppled.

So, after a lifelong interest in politics, I finally set my mind to fighting a serious campaign to be an MP. It was my working-class background and exposure to the healthy political divide in my own family that had brought me to this point.

I was born in Stockport in 1960. Dad was a 'fitter' at a local engineering factory and Mum worked as a dinner lady at St George's Church of England primary school. Like many of their generation, my parents had never had the opportunity to take advantage of a full secondary education. Mill work beckoned for Mum and Dad also had to get out and earn a living. Mum read voraciously. For years and years she would be reading four or five books at the same time. One of my earliest memories is trooping alongside her as a small boy to the local library in Gladstone Street. She read every-thing – autobiographies, biographies, fiction, history, the lot. As I was emerging into adolescence, Dad also started to read. His chief interest was anything to do with modern history, politics and the war. Add to this mix of background reading the fact that both Mum and Dad were very opinionated about all things political and you can see the cauldron of ideas and debate that was my family home. Mum was essentially liberal; Dad was socialist, veering slightly towards

Communism and then becoming quite right wing in his later life.

This was an era when there were striking differences between the main political parties. Labour could actually be called socialist, the Liberals were liberal and the Conservatives – well, in my neck of the woods they were referred to in language not suitable for this book. There seemed to be so much more current affairs on the television. Even trade union conferences were televised on the few major national channels. There were characters like Jo Gormley of the National Union of Miners, who could be seen taking his jacket off, rolling up his sleeves and striding down the main hall to deal with a politician who had strayed off message. Nowadays, I think they'd get a text on their Blackberry.

It would be quite normal for me and Mum and Dad to be calmly watching the news with our teas on our laps, when suddenly Mum would start heckling the person on the TV. Inevitably, Dad would join in, and before you knew where you were there was a full-blown row going on. If the chairs had been green and we had painted a red line down each side of the room, we could have been in the Commons at 58 Dial Park Road.

Grammar school and university, both in Manchester, led to my first job as a research scientist for Philips. Here I grew semiconductor slices. As the name suggests, this was not exactly riveting. I remember having to wear a white coat. Having attended a number of leaving dos where people were given a gold clock for wearing a white coat for twenty-five years, I decided that I had to spread my wings, leave my home area and see the world.

I ended up convincing myself that I should join the RAF. I like aeroplanes and had a sense that RAF officer training would be a challenge. Having completed the cut-out coupon on the 'Join the RAF' advert in the *Daily Mail*, I was duly dropped off at RAF College Cranwell to start my officer training on 5 February 1984 at 5 p.m. Why is my recollection of the date and time so precise? Because within days I realised that this was the moment I had done probably the single most stupid thing I'd ever done in my life. Let's just say that my aspiration to find RAF officer training a challenge was met in full. In fact, the mixture of sheer physical exertion, mental stress, sleep-deprivation and downright terror of the drill instructor did at times feel life-threatening. My sisters still recoil in fits of laughter when they remember my plaintive calls for help from the little red telephone box outside the guard room of RAF College Cranwell. The trials and tribulations of this period in my life would fill a book of their own. I can probably give you a flavour by recounting just one of the many exchanges between myself and my drill instructor: 'Student Officer Carroll, you are like a lighthouse in the desert – bright but useless.' He could have given master classes in the cutting put down.

After a brief six-year career in the RAF, specialising

in radar systems that detected Russian aircraft during the Cold War, I moved on to run a technology company for the University of Durham.

Then in 1992, my brother-in-law Colin – with whom I had always got on well, to the point that I would regard him as a brother rather than an in-law – suggested that I might want to join him and build up the successful road transport business that he had run with my sister Brenda for many years. This involved a move to Kent. By now I was thirty-two and it was at this point that I felt it was time to really set out my stall and attempt to become an MP.

So why not Labour? This was the era of 'New Labour'. The Labour Party that I had grown up following had been utterly and completely changed by the efforts of Peter Mandelson and Tony Blair. I recall that some-one once quipped, 'Old Labour was principled but unelectable; New Labour was unprincipled but electa-ble'. As one-liners go, it's amusing and sharp, though I'm sure it oversimplifies the situation. That said, I had sympathy with the many Labour-leaning people who felt that in its desire to become electable, the Labour Party effectively changed itself into something more akin to the Tories; a kind of Conservative Party-lite. For me, the Labour Party at that time seemed like a child in the playground trying to change its behaviour to be liked. It just didn't work. The Liberal Democrats, meanwhile, seemed genuinely rooted in their passion for the individual. Call me idealistic, but the Lib Dems always seemed sympathetic to the underdog, with a healthy scepticism that government didn't always know best.

It all goes back to those childhood memories: the realisation that for a great many people life is really tough, the deep understanding that there is an inherent unfairness when people like Mum and Dad were denied the chances they should have had. Even for me, going to grammar school left a curious mark on my personality. There was a feeling that somehow I was an outsider coming from the working class, an unstated undercurrent that somehow the opportunities were for the sons and daughters of doctors, dentists, the 'professional' classes.

At that time, and indeed for most of my time actively fighting to become an MP as a Lib Dem, I genuinely saw my party as the one that understood that standing up for the 'have nots' is a good thing. That fighting for fairness and equality of opportunity for people of all backgrounds was the right way forward. It may sound naive, but every time I saw young people from the east side of Folkestone, I saw myself.

Having polled a respectable 15,000 votes to gain a strong second place against Michael Howard's 20,000 in the 2001 general election, I was using all my spare time to build up a campaign to take him on again in the election of 2005.

I had always taken the view that the best MPs were the ones who 'worked their patch' as candidates. These would be the ones who immersed themselves in their local area and actually fought to change things that were causing people problems. So many MPs go a different route. There is an almost cynical analysis of where the 'safest' seat is and many, many MPs win their seat more because of the party that they stand for than because they have won the hearts and minds of local people. With that in mind, I was always trying to help people with problems, be they benefit issues, planning matters or a multitude of other issues.

In 2004 I received a call from Brian Staley, a hard-working Lib Dem activist in Canterbury. Brian, who I did not then know well, said something about Gurkha soldiers and immigration and how 'it all seemed wrong'. I couldn't quite absorb his central point, but agreed that he should send over the four retired Gurkhas who had approached him and on whose behalf he had called.

The Gurkhas arrived at my Folkestone home on a Sunday afternoon. They were very smart and polite. As is their custom, they removed their shoes upon entering the house. They sat in the lounge and slowly and deliberately explained the situation in which they found themselves. Before me were Gopal Giri, Bhim, Bidur Pakhrin and Prem Limbu.

Living in the Folkestone area you are very aware of the Gurkha presence. The Gurkhas moved to Folkestone in 2000 and it is now their main base. There are approximately 3,500 Gurkhas serving in the British Army, with several hundred at their main Folkestone base at any time. They are a common sight running and training in the local area. A number of businesses have emerged locally to supply their particular wants and a local shop has been turned into a little bit of the Himalayas – Gurkha Hill on Risborough Lane. You will often drive down Cheriton High Street and suddenly, amongst the grey Western dress of the locals, see a blaze of luminous green and bright red as the Gurkha mothers take their children to school or go shopping.

Apart from just knowing that the Gurkhas were around, the only knowledge I had of them was handed down to me by my father. He had explained something of their history and how it was defined by the most exceptional loyalty, devotion and valour.

My four visitors started to explain their predicament. Essentially, it was this: under the rules applied by successive British governments, retired Gurkhas were always discharged from the British Army back in Nepal and were not allowed a right of settlement in the UK. The government traced this ruling back to the controversial 1947 Tripartite Agreement between India, the UK and Nepal. This ruling meant that even the Gurkhas talking to me now technically had no right to stay in Britain. The 1947 agreement had been drawn up when India gained independence, prior to which many Gurkhas had served in the British Indian Army. The British government was keen to maintain a Gurkha contingent in the British Army and many Gurkhas would continue to serve in India as part of the Indian Army; therefore, the three nations involved in the situation needed to formalise the arrangements under which Gurkhas could be recruited. The key provisions of the 1947 agreement were that Gurkhas would be recruited in Nepal and discharged in Nepal. As a result of the rigid application of this agreement, Gurkha soldiers were sent back to Nepal to be discharged. And since there was no right of entry to the UK, they could normally only get back to Britain under tightly controlled visitor visa arrangements. It was this point of 'discharge' that was to be used by the British government as a means of blocking our campaign.

Some who did return under the provision of visitor visas 'overstayed' and then applied to enter Britain. Those that did were forced to live in a 'grey area', fearful of negative comparisons with 'illegal immigrants'. Almost all wanted to work in the UK, but were not allowed to by law. Nor were they allowed any access to public funds or benefits, not that they wanted them – work was the preferred option.

Gopal Giri, Bhim, Bidur Pakhrin and Prem Limbu told me that their colleague, Tej Limbu, a retired Gurkha with thirteen years' service, had been arrested and taken to Dover deportation centre to be forcibly deported back to Nepal on a flight from Heathrow.

As they explained the issue I recall the immense feeling of shock, not at hearing that all retired Gurkhas were expected to go back to Nepal, but that they would then not be able to return to the UK to settle. Then I remember my shock giving way to incredulity – to the point where I felt the need to double-check that they had actually got their facts right. Indeed they

10

had: no retired Gurkha had the automatic right to live in Britain.

The four men told me that they were part of the Brigade of Gurkha Welfare Society (BGWS), a charity established by retired Gurkhas to help the retired Gurkha community. They explained that they had been to see their local MP, my adversary Michael Howard, and that he had been unsympathetic to their plea that they should have the right to stay in Britain. Rather outrageously, in my view, he had suggested that they apply for asylum if they really wanted to stay. This they took as more of an insult than an offer of help: they wanted the right to remain as a direct consequence of their service, not as the result of an expedient asylum claim. Michael Howard subsequently issued a press release explaining that retired Gurkhas should go back to Nepal – only to hastily recall it and explain it away as a mistake when challenged on the local BBC Radio Kent.

I spent many hours pondering how best to help. By now I had the experience of building up my own election campaign and, whilst trying to help local people, I had run several small campaigns on local matters such as the closure of local post offices. This issue was different. It had a national, indeed international, dimension. It would be relatively easy to express outrage at this situation and perhaps get a few column inches in the local newspaper. But it would be much more difficult to put together what would be needed to actually change this situation. How would I even start? *Where* would I start?

Lying in the bath, I spent many hours thinking this through. Was it even remotely achievable? Could the country's Lib Dems help? Should I go to the national press? There was a problem with that: I didn't know how to even go about it.

I'm not a great football fan. However, the one tournament that catches my imagination is the FA Cup. I find the matches where you see Crawley Town taking on Manchester United captivating. Right now I was feeling like Crawley Town taking on Barcelona!

I researched the subject extensively on the internet. The Gurkhas were not without friends. A number of MPs had spoken up for them in Parliament, most notably Ann Widdecombe, the MP for Maidstone & The Weald. She had participated in several debates on the issue and pressed ministers for action. I admired her for taking stand.

I now became aware that the Gurkhas had formed a number of separate, very separate, campaigning groups. There was the Gurkha Army Ex-Serviceman's Organisation (GAESO), the United British Gurkhas Ex-Army (UBGEA) and the BGWS, to name but three. Over the ensuing years, I was to discover just how fractured the retired Gurkha community really was. Speaking and working with one group could easily lead to another group no longer speaking or communicating with you. There were constant accusations from each group about every other group. Any attempt to really try and understand these myriad inter-group conflicts would end in complete befuddlement. The situation became a little clearer when it was explained to me by some of my Gurkha friends that back in Nepal there are 200 political parties, not the handful that we are used to dealing with in the UK, and that, as a consequence, unity is sometimes a victim in the Nepali culture. Part of the problem was the underlying divisions between different clans back in Nepal. Another was the fact that some groups very definitely reflected different ranks within the Gurkhas. I found that every group seemed totally sincere. All my early campaigning work on this issue was alongside the BGWS. At one point, I spoke with the GEASO. They had approached me and said that they wanted advice on how to campaign and I freely gave it. Immediately all contact with the BGWS ceased. Gurkha members of the BGWS with whom I had spent many, many hours cut me dead. This felt extraordinary. Faced with this, I took refuge in the view that Gurkhas were Gurkhas and that I would help any and all that approached me. Repeatedly I explained that in British public life, campaigns that have a united front have a greater chance of success and at one point I urged each of the main groups to forge an alliance. This they attempted by forming an 'umbrella group'. I attended a couple of pretty feisty meetings during this period.

My only option was to stay above any conflict of this kind. When faced with a powerful foe, in this case the Ministry of Defence (MoD), the Home Office and pretty much every other part of the British establishment, such in-fighting on our side was a huge distraction and it damaged our overall ability to campaign. We even had situations at some of the rallies and demonstrations outside Parliament and in Whitehall where groups that had decided not to take part would suddenly appear and we almost had fights. And that's after the police responsible for public order in Whitehall had expressed their joy at having Gurkha events because there was never any chance of trouble – little did they know.

I knew that the media would be a crucial component of any campaign with any hope of changing this situation. The very next day I decided to take my first steps to try and get the Gurkha issue into the public arena. But how to do it?

I used Directory Enquiries to get the number for the BBC and fought their internal switchboard to get through to their newsroom. Eventually, having been passed from pillar to post, I received a call from Nick, one of the production team on the *Jeremy Vine Show*.

Within days, I was on BBC Radio 2 with one of the four retired Gurkhas, Bidur Pakhrin. We did the show down an ISDN line – a special phone line that makes you sound as if you are actually in the London studio with the presenter – from our local BBC studio in Tunbridge Wells. Bidur and I were huddled in the tiny telephone kiosk of a studio wearing headphones the size of ear defenders. Suddenly, the line came alive and a powerful calm voice said: 'This is BBC Control at the centre – can you hear us?' It sounded like a line out of *Star Trek*.

I'd done Radio Kent many times during my local campaigning work in and around Folkestone, but this was my first experience of the BBC on a national scale. For some reason I asked, nervously, 'How many people will be listening?'

BBC Central Control came back: 'Hard to say but around six million.'

This enormous number made me gulp, but I thought it was going to make Bidur faint.

Jeremy Vine was gentle with us. I now know that the BBC received huge positive feedback on the issue and the *Daily Express* took the issue straight to its front page, with James Slack covering the story.

Powerful as it is, the media on its own doesn't change things. This issue needed a political component if it was to succeed. But for now, our media campaign had begun.

BIDUR PAKHRIN

Bidur was one of the four retired Gurkhas who had come to my home to ask for my help, and since he lived in Cheriton, about one mile away from me, it made logistical sense for him to be my main point of contact as I grappled with how we should best embark on this campaign. In so many ways, Bidur encapsulated the issue. He had left the Gurkhas and settled a few miles from the barracks in Cheriton. He had managed to do this even though he had no 'right' to stay in Britain. He had succeeded in getting a job driving an HGV for a transport company in a village called Lypmne, not far from Folkestone, and he and his family were supporting themselves. But they lived in constant fear of the 'knock on the door' from the immigration authorities. It was desperately sad that he couldn't ever risk leaving the country for fear of not being able to re-enter at the airport. Tragically, during this period one of his parents became ill and Bidur, despite having an immaculate service record with the Gurkhas, could not go and support his family back in Nepal – if he had, he might never again have been able to come back to Britain. Such were the terrible stresses we inflicted on the people who had worn our uniform.

TWO

LIVERPOOL AND BOURNEMOUTH

———•———

L iverpool is not the most obvious choice for a major demonstration. However, before my involvement, the BGWS had decided that 1 September 2004 would see the city play host to the first in what was to become a long line of lobbies, marches and petitions. I understood the logic that had led to this decision: a number of Home Office departments that were looking into Gurkha settlement issues were located there. The national press, however, are not. My advice, if I'd been involved earlier, would have been to stage this demonstration in central London – in Whitehall, outside Parliament or even outside the Home Office. The media work to a frenetic schedule: changes to their priorities and plans come thick and fast, and even for the big players such as the BBC, ITV and Sky there is a finite number of crews and cameras. As most political events are centred on the capital, it is inevitable that London-based events get more coverage. But by this stage plans were too far advanced to be changed – Liverpool it would have to be.

The organisational force behind the Liverpool event was Tikendra Dewan, the leader of the BGWS. Our relationship was to deteriorate dramatically as the campaign developed, but in the early days he and his team worked very closely with me. Tikendra and the BGWS are based over in Hampshire, a natural consequence of the many Gurkhas serving and then settling there. It is an impressive organisation. They operate from a building in Farnborough and have set up a number of community support projects to help with legal and social matters of which I feel they should be justifiably proud. Tikendra is articulate, with a complete grasp of the issues and the organisational skills to be effective. He achieved high rank in the Gurkhas and managed to get the right to settle in Britain. This was exceptional. He was now working as a civil servant for a division of the Ministry of Defence.

Tikendra and his team had arranged for about 400 retired Gurkhas to travel by coach to Liverpool. I decided to make my own way there by car. I had so much to do back in Folkestone & Hythe that I planned to drive all the way up, attend the event, and then drive straight back.

Now these were the days before Sat Nav was so widely available. I drove straight into the heart of

Liverpool and tried to find the government offices amongst that morass of ring roads and one-way streets that makes all city centres a nightmare for infrequent visitors. I had travelled up with my constituency organiser, Miranda, who had helped make us some placards, and I was stopped at a set of lights when she spotted exactly where we needed to be – right behind us. The lights went green and though there were plenty of signs prohibiting the manoeuvre, I shouted out, 'We're doing a U-ey!' My passengers shrieked and held on for dear life as I flung the car around and finally got us to where we needed to be.

As it happened, we arrived ahead of the Gurkhas and were able to position ourselves, slightly self-consciously, outside the government buildings. There we awaited the main infantry.

They arrived in a fleet of coaches. As the months and years would unfold, I was to attend many such gatherings, but this was the first time that I had seen a mass gathering of retired Gurkhas. They were wearing what was effectively their 'retired' uniform – a green blazer, beige trousers and the iconic Gurkha hat. As they emerged from their coaches and began to mill about outside the building, I was struck by their demeanour. The Gurkhas have a warmth about them that just attracts good feeling and support. The fine people of Liverpool were now stopping to talk. Passing motorists tooted in support. Some locals even asked if they could hold one of our placards and stand with us. The Gurkhas were just incredibly polite and gentle.

All we had done was to start helping them to discover the power of the media and the need to organise and fight their cause as if it were a battle, but even at this early stage everyone had a smile and good wishes for us.

Tikendra was to head a small delegation which would meet senior Home Office officials. It hadn't been arranged for me to attend but I offered to go in, an offer that Tikendra accepted.

The meeting took place in a grand, imposing room. High ceilings and majestic windows. The centre piece of the room was the sort of expansive dark wooden table around which you could imagine the great city merchants deliberating over maritime charts as they planned world domination. There were no politicians present – these were senior civil servants.

The atmosphere was tense. The officials made their contributions to the discussion in carefully measured language that called to mind a chess player moving pieces across the board. Classic civil service speak: each word and phrase deliberated over and precisely delivered. They outlined the current position – polite, but giving nothing away. We were informed that the government was currently 'reviewing' the situation relating to Gurkha settlement and that some kind of announcement might be imminent.

Tikendra set out his case extremely well and the meeting ended with polite handshakes all round, but I was left feeling slightly awkward, frustrated that my lack of an in-depth understanding of the situation prevented me from contributing to the discussion with confidence. Every fibre of my being told me that this state of affairs was patently and totally unfair, but at this stage in the campaign I was not yet familiar with all the nuances of law that made it so.

The immaculately turned out Gurkhas waiting outside were full of expectancy. Tikendra reported what had been said. Then I offered to say a few words. And there, on the streets of Liverpool, I made my first real old fashioned political speech, as I imagine might have happened in the past. If I had had a soap box I would have used it. I found myself telling the listening crowd just how bad this situation made me feel as a British citizen. That we needed to fight this 'tooth and nail'. That this would be a mammoth struggle with setbacks all the way and that we would have to use every public, legal and political weapon that we could find.

But, for me, it was not what I said. It was how it made me feel looking out at that sea of faces. They were standing politely and attentively, yet looking back on it that was the moment that I really felt their pain and suffering – the look on their faces was almost haunting.

———•———

With Liverpool behind us, it was time to press on.

Charles Kennedy was then the leader of the Liberal Democrats. I did not know him well but he had visited me in Folkestone & Hythe in the final days before the 2001 General Election, so I made contact with his office and he very kindly agreed to meet with the retired Gurkhas and hear what they had to say. After the meeting, Kennedy took the matter to the floor of the House of Commons at Prime Minister's Questions and then, when I decided that I needed to raise the issue at the Liberal Democrat Federal Conference in Bournemouth in September 2004, I found that I had his full support. Without doubt, Charles Kennedy was the first party leader to take the issue seriously.

In years gone by, party conferences were truly events of national importance. During the Labour and Conservative (and subsequently the Liberal Democrat) conferences there were often fierce debates that could really influence policy. However, in more modern times all the main party conferences tend to be strictly stage-managed by the party administration. That said, party conferences are still important for other reasons. It is the one time that the party physically comes together and the activists and workers meet and mingle with the MPs. So the media watch proceedings very carefully, on the lookout for any whiff of a split, scandal or a significant change in direction. Getting the Gurkha issue on the party conference agenda would give the campaign a shot at further media coverage.

With that in mind, I began the fraught process of talking with the conference organisers to get clearance for an 'emergency motion' calling for Gurkhas to have the right of settlement. Party managers spend a great deal of time making sure that the conference agenda is as free of pitfalls as possible: there is always the risk that a motion could make it through to the floor of the conference that a hostile media could then pounce on and trash. For the Lib Dems the danger always seems to lie in debates titled 'Abolish the Monarchy' or 'Legalise Drugs'. Now, these issues are undoubtedly serious matters. There are people – not just in political parties – who have strong views on either side of both issues. In a rational world, this should make them suitable subjects for debate. However, we don't live in a rational world – certainly not when it comes to the media. Any discussion on topics like these would lead to rabid headlines in the popular press. And so, whilst they may not admit it publicly, all the main parties invest considerable bureaucratic energy in thwarting any group that tries to get these issues debated at conference.

I spent the morning trying to track down the various committee members who might be able to help me get the Gurkha issue allowed as an emergency motion. Unbelievably, some questioned whether it was really an 'emergency'. I was getting frustrated: 'If you're a Gurkha veteran with fifteen years' service and you're living on a settee in Ruislip barred from working and fearing deportation – you might find that a bit of an emergency,' was my retort.

I suffered a whole morning of trying to remain calm with people who seemed not to understand how important this issue was. I knew that to appear too forceful and critical of them would put their backs up and make my job harder. I argued that this was an issue with which the general public would have a great deal of sympathy. Compared to some of the no doubt worthy but dry as dust debate that goes on at conference, here was something that might be popular in the eyes of the nation. This was the first time that I detected a strange mental condition that seems to affect many politicians – they fight all their lives for popularity in order to get elected, but then, when a golden opportunity arises which will make them popular, they find ten reasons why they can't do it!

Finally, the carpet in the Bournemouth International Conference Centre completely worn out, I succeeded in securing the inclusion of the Gurkha issue as an emergency motion. The slot allocated for the debate was in the early afternoon.

Bidur Pakhrin, my co-star on the *Jeremy Vine Show*, had been tasked with bringing down a group of Gurkha veterans to attend the debate, but as the scheduled time grew nearer, still the Gurkhas had not appeared. By now I was making increasingly anxious mobile phone calls – the first of innumerable experiences of having to do the lobbying, organise the waiting media and generally keep the show on the road. When at last they arrived, the rules were waived to allow Tikendra Dewan to address the conference and his fellow Gurkhas. The hall was packed.

Tikendra spoke brilliantly, as he had in Liverpool, and Paul Keetch, the party's spokesman on defence, also took to the floor to champion the cause. Incredibly, the motion was carried with total support.

Conference is, by its nature, a predominantly sedate affair. For large parts of the sessions it murmurs along, punctuated occasionally by the mass movements of people in and out as the topic for debate changes. But when the Gurkha motion was passed, conference reacted with an almost literal wave of emotion. As the Gurkhas stood up to leave, the hall rose as one to salute them. Some were moved to tears. The veterans left the hall to the stirring sound of Gurkha pipes and a swelling chorus of applause.

A very moving day, and the second of our first two steps on a long political road.

THREE

FIRST BREAKTHROUGH, SETBACKS AND TURMOIL

————•————

I n September 2004 the Blair government declared that the rules about settlement rights for retired Gurkhas were to be radically changed. Many have kindly said that this decision was a direct result of the pressure that I and others had brought to bear; others said it merely helped a little on the way. Some of my political opponents in the Folkestone area dismissed my work during 2004 as having no impact at all.

The Prime Minister and the Home Secretary, David Blunkett, announced that Gurkhas who retired after July 1997 were to be given the right to apply to settle in the UK as citizens. For a small number of retired Gurkhas this change would bring welcome relief; for the majority, however, it brought nothing but abject despair and outraged rejection – those who retired before 1997 still could not apply to live in the UK.

The government defended the 1997 cut-off date on the basis that prior to this date the Gurkhas were based in Hong Kong and appeared to suggest that in some way this meant they weren't part of Home Forces. These were the veterans of the first Gulf War, the Falklands War, Malaya and, of course, the Second World War.

The removal of this 1997 cut-off date became the central aim of what turned into the Gurkha Justice campaign.

I was on a short break in the south of France when the news broke. I felt a curious mixture of jubilation that some progress had been made and an emerging and growing sense of anger that the retired Gurkha community was to be divided into post- and pre-1997 retirees.

I did a couple of radio interviews by mobile phone and on one station Bidur Pakhrin spoke with me. When asked by the radio interviewer, 'How do you feel?' Bidur replied, 'How can I feel any joy when my brothers in arms are still left out?' His answer summed up how we all felt.

But for me, the focus of my campaigning life had by necessity switched back to my fight for the seat of Folkestone & Hythe.

The turmoil in the leadership of the Conservative Party had led to a dramatic change in Mr Howard's position. He was now Party Leader. From a possible sunset phase on the back benches he was now catapulted to the top party position. Taking him on as leader would be in a whole new league of difficulty. For a high profile MP to lose his seat would be embarrassing for both the MP and his party. For a party to lose its leader would be unthinkable. It would be a sensation and a catastrophe. Faced with this as even an outside possibility, the Conservative Party would undoubtedly deploy massive resources to defend him. They would spend a lot of money in the run-up to the election in order to boost his support: canvassing, taking polls to check how the campaign was going and then deploying even more leaflets, letters and other resources if the results suggested even the slightest chance of him being embarrassed.

From our side, I remember thinking at the time that my bid might well resemble the Charge of the Light Brigade – and so it was to prove – however, I had committed to the seat and generated a strong level of support in the 2001 general election. Buoyed by this result, I had pressed on and gained even more local backing, and if the relatively high Labour vote of 10,000 in the 2001 general election could now be persuaded to swing behind me in 2005, it could very well be a close-run thing.

The Lib Dems are very much a 'bottom up' movement. Most Lib Dem MPs have to work hard to build up their local support. They need to gather around them hundreds of people who are prepared to canvass for them, deliver leaflets on their behalf, put up posters at election time and do the one hundred and one other things that need to be done when fighting an election. As well as that, they need to have with them people who really know how to organise this great mass of volunteers and manage everything involved in an effective campaign. I was very fortunate to have two of the most effective election agents and the campaign organisers in the Lib Dem world with me in Folkestone & Hythe. Shaun Roberts and Miranda Piercy were exceptionally gifted people and they had committed to helping me 'build to win'.

Largely as a result of the skills of Shaun and Miranda and the phenomenal hard work of hundreds of volunteers, we had built up a very powerful Lib Dem organisation in Folkestone & Hythe, and in 2003 we achieved massive gains in the local elections at district council level and at individual town council level.

Local election results are not a guide to how a general election result will go in the same area. That said, it is pretty much a truism that Lib Dem MPs only get elected if there is a strong showing at local election level. Just to give you an idea, the ultra Conservative town of Hythe had always had a town council that was dominated by the Conservatives. Typically, over past decades, they would have held fourteen of the sixteen seats, with the Lib Dems holding the other two. After the local elections of 2003 we had taken fourteen seats and the Conservatives were left with two. It was as if the roof of Hythe Town Hall had been rent asunder.

Howard was a backbencher, their local representation had been mauled and the Lib Dems had taken 50 per cent of the vote. These were the classic signs that a once safe Tory seat was becoming vulnerable to a major 'mother of all campaigns' fight from the Lib Dems at the next general election.

And then disaster struck. Not some great national catastrophe but a local one. On the back of monumental grassroots campaigning we elected a massive majority of Lib Dem councillors onto Shepway District Council. The Lib Dems were in control. Shepway District Council covers the same area as the parliamentary constituency of Folkestone & Hythe. As seems ever to be the case, local government finances were under pressure and the new Lib Dem administration had to grapple with some difficult figures. Shaun, Miranda and I knew this would pose some difficulties, but we felt secure in the knowledge that amongst the newly elected councillors were several who had been involved in local government for decades, some of whom had actually run the authority some years previously. We satisfied ourselves with the thought that there was a mixture of new, enthusiastic councillors and experienced old hands, and that they would make a good job of running the council – or a passable one, at least. How wrong we were.

Within months the Lib Dem administration on Shepway District Council destroyed any hope I had of having a realistic chance against Michael Howard in the 2005 general election. Faced with financial pressure, they lost all sense of reality and any political reason. They shut every public toilet, attempted to raise the council tax by 38 per cent (before being capped by the government at 20 per cent) and stopped looking after the public areas and open spaces in the district. Total and absolute disaster. Eventually, under the combination of financial and local political pressure, the Lib Dem administration collapsed with recrimination everywhere. Strong friendships were shattered and so much good work and progress were lost. It was awful.

Just as a prospective MP can benefit from the good things that local councillors do, so too do they reap the whirlwind when their local colleagues get it all so badly wrong. As I went about the business of campaigning during 2004, the public mood turned savagely. Instead of praise for the many local initiatives and case work that I was doing for local people, people were now telling me that the performance of the local council was so disastrous that they wouldn't vote Lib Dem ever again at any level. The dead hand of local Conservative control was re-established and Howard was safe.

Fighting with absolute commitment and intensity against such odds was utterly exhausting. However, hundreds of local people had worked for me and had faith in me. I felt deeply that I had to go through with it out of loyalty to them and because of the fact that I don't think of myself as a quitter. If they play *My Way* at my funeral, it will be for the line 'I bit off more than I could chew'!

The Gurkha story ran throughout all of this local political turmoil. Dozens of retired Gurkhas helped me in my desperate struggle to fight a respectable campaign against Michael Howard MP. And all the while the injustice of the pre-1997 Gurkha retirees remained unresolved. We had to fight on.

MADAN KUNAR GURUNG

I am Madan Kunar Gurung. I have three children: one daughter and two sons. I joined the British Army on 24 November 1969, served for twenty-four years and retired in March 1993. In 2004 settlement rights were given to Gurkhas in the UK. When I heard that all ex-Gurkhas were now allowed to stay in the UK, I came with my wife to settle here on 21 January 2007. I applied for my settlement to the Home Office in February 2007. After thirteen months of waiting, I was refused on the grounds that I had no strong ties with this country. I was very upset, angry and depressed. During this period of waiting we were not allowed to work or receive any benefit, but we approached the Royal British Legion, who supported us, giving a little money and some food vouchers.

In February 2008 I heard that there was a meeting in Folkestone community hall about the Gurkhas. I took my wife and at the end of the meeting I was given a chance to say a few words about my refusal from the Home Office and how we were waiting for the settlement right. During our waiting period we had to ask friends to give us shelter and we were moving every month from one place to another; sometimes every three months, sometimes two. I cried in this meeting as I explained the difficulties we were getting into to English friends whom I did not yet know.

At the end of the meeting a couple came to see us and they listened to our problem. They were Peter

Carroll and his wife, Lynne Beaumount. They both promised to help and support us. Peter Carroll took us and gave us a two-bedroom house to stay in in Kent, Maidstone.

I think that this is the day that God came for all the Gurkha veterans – the day I met Peter and Lynne. From this day Peter started his campaign for the Gurkhas. They took us to Parliament and various corners and places of the country, day or night, campaigning for the Gurkhas. He got actresses Joanna Lumley and Virginia McKenna involved in the campaign. Peter Carroll fought for the Gurkhas for nearly six years. Without Peter Carroll, the Gurkha Veterans would never have won the right to settle in the United Kingdom. Peter Carroll, Lynne Beaumount and Joanna Lumley will never be forgotten by the Gurkha veterans.

The Gurkha Justice campaign is highly appreciated by all the Gurkha veterans. Today all the Gurkhas you see in the United Kingdom are the fruit of the Gurkha Justice campaign.

FOUR

THE MIDDLE YEARS

———◆———

By March 2007 we had decided to hold a major rally to kick start a new phase of the campaign. We wrote to every MP and every member of the House of Lords to tell them that we would be gathering in Parliament Square. Every parliamentarian received an invitation to come out on the day and sign a 'Pledge Board'. This was an idea that just came into my head one evening, probably when I was in the bath. It occurred to me that we would be demonstrating outside Parliament, but the very people we needed to influence would be inside, not out – so why not invite the parliamentarians out to meet us? After all, it was a pretty short walk. A potential logistical difficulty arose when we considered how exactly to get a large white board safely and easily to the square, but in the end a bit of Gurkha ingenuity came to the rescue. We actually used a big white sheet, complete with a black marker for use by those who braved the traffic and crossed into the square.

To their great credit, many did come out. Others made use of an enclosed reply slip to indicate their view on the matter of Gurkha pensions and settlement rights. Baroness Trumpington stomped across the grass and, in an imperious manner, demanded that she be able to sign swiftly: 'Trumpington here. Where do I sign?' All very House of Lords! Ann Widdecombe signed our pledge and talked movingly about the shameful 1997 cut-off date. Baroness Harris, who had spoken in support of my motion at the 2004 Lib Dem conference, also signed up.

Our plan was to leave Parliament Square at an appointed hour and march up Whitehall to the Cenotaph before moving on to the Gurkha memorial outside the Ministry of Defence. As would become usual, the police from Charing Cross had worked with us to help plan the day. Marching and protesting within a mile of Westminster is now covered by the provisions of the Serious Organised Crime and Police Act (SOCPA). This controversial piece of legislation, with which we had to comply on numerous occasions, states that anyone wishing to demonstrate in a prescribed area around Whitehall must inform the Metropolitan Police, who then have the right to put 'conditions' on the event. These conditions might relate to the length of time the event can take or the number of people that can attend. The police can also set out terms relating to stewarding and other safety matters associated with the demonstration.

Allegedly, the intention of SOCPA was to ensure that the police had enough time to try and plan for protests in this sensitive area. To this day, some see it as an affront to the right to demonstrate and many people, myself included, think it very un-British to have to inform a police officer before protesting. On occasions, the enforcement of SOCPA has been farcical. One lady was arrested because she sat on Parliament Square and ate a cake with the word 'PEACE' on it. The revealing of the cake and its subsequent consumption was viewed as an 'unauthorised' demonstration. In a more sinister example, a woman was arrested for reading out the names of the Iraq War dead on the steps of the Cenotaph.

There are two men who are particular thorns in the side of the SOCPA establishment. The first is comedian and activist Mark Thomas. Allegedly, he became the scourge of the Charing Cross police events team charged with looking after demonstrations by performing innumerable 'one man' protests day after day, each requiring the police to go through the long process of considering the application, filling out the forms and setting the relevant 'conditions'. The second was Brian Haw and his rough, tented village right outside Parliament. Almost every shot of Whitehall featured his tent and flagpole with its many signs criticising the government for pretty much everything to do with Iraq and then Afghanistan. The courts ruled that since he had started demonstrating before SOCPA was passed the police had no right to move him. He was there for years and years, until his death in 2011. Now that is British.

One of the great supporters of our campaign and with it from the early days was Darren Briddock, stalwart of the Folkestone & Hythe Liberal Democrats. Darren has an imposing physical presence. He is tall – and when surrounded by a sea of retired Gurkhas he looks even taller. On many of our events Darren was at the forefront, setting the pace for marches and herding the streams of retired Gurkhas into parade-like formations. Now, with Darren taking the lead, our long column snaked its way around the outer edge of Parliament Square to the customary, and very welcome, hoots of support from passing cars and lorries.

With the police helicopter clattering overhead, our great crowd of retired Gurkhas filed into Whitehall. PC McInally, a doughty Scot so often the policeman in charge of such matters, walked at the front with Darren. We had been expressly told that we must ensure all the people on the parade would behave in an acceptable manner in Whitehall, and particularly near the Cenotaph. As we approached the designated area, PC McInally was growling in his Scottish accent, telling everyone to stay behind the lines that delineate the Cenotaph.

What happened next could only be described as 'not our finest hour'. The distracting and totally unhelpful rivalry between different groups of retired Gurkhas had threatened the day almost from the start. Representatives from the GAESO and the BGWS were both present and there had been barely suppressed disputes around which of the banners from these different groups should be at the front of the campaign. The prospect of Gurkhas in open conflict with each other in front of the media would be a PR disaster for our cause. And now, suddenly, the Gurkhas broke ranks and were everywhere. Some stood on the Cenotaph steps: absolutely prohibited. Much worse was to come as a megaphone was produced. Darren could see PC McInally's hands flirting over his handcuffs. To this day, I'm not sure who he was going to arrest first – me, as event organiser (although, looking at the scene unfolding before me, 'organiser' was potentially an exaggeration) or Darren, who was closer. In Nepali culture respects are paid quite differently and cheering and applause are entirely acceptable at acts of remembrance. Looking at the expression on PC McInally's face, I was convinced that cultural flexibility did not extend to Scottish PCs in the Met.

Somehow, and I genuinely can't recall how, Darren and I managed to assert some kind of order and we moved on up Whitehall, turning right just past the Ministry of Defence to the Gurkha memorial. So large was the crowd that I had to stand on a window ledge to address the throng.

The veterans minister, Derek Twigg MP, had agreed to meet us. This was to be my first ministerial meeting on the issue. I left the crowd outside and went into the building along with Tikendra Dewan of the BGWS and the wonderful added boost of Betty Boothroyd. Lady Boothroyd had responded to our earlier letter and expressed her wish to support us; I suggested that attending this meeting with the minister might be the best way for her to do so.

The meeting with the minister was challenging. Tikendra and I, accompanied by Lady Boothroyd, went through security at MoD main reception and were escorted through the vast open-plan offices that spread like the prairies through the massive building. Eventually, we reached the minister's office.

Mr Twigg was cordial. He was flanked by a very smart looking female civil servant. Tikendra and I set out our main concerns: the appalling pensions paid to retired Gurkhas and the divisive 1997 cut-off date relating to settlement rights. The government had just announced some changes to the Gurkha pension system that would mean a better deal, but again only for Gurkhas who retired after 1997.

Lady Boothroyd was formidable. Her first call to me had been typical of the lady. She had called my mobile and veritably bellowed down the phone: 'This is Boothroyd – I want Peter Carroll. Is that you?' It put the fear of God in me, and I knew then how she had commanded the House when she was Speaker. Now, she used this same force to press the minister into clarifying certain points relating to the level of Gurkha pensions. He was explaining his point when, quick as a flash, Lady Boothroyd whipped a copy of Hansard out of her handbag. It was slightly rolled up and for one unnerving moment I thought she might actually hit him with it, just like a stereotypical angry wife might deal with a husband late home from the pub. His current answer appeared to contradict something he had said that she remembered from a previous debate. The minister was visibly shaken.

I probed him a different way. I was trying to ascertain just how fixed the government was in its view on the overall issue. Changing tack, I asked the minister how he felt as a human being presiding over a system that paid retired Gurkhas about one-sixth of the pension earned by an equivalent UK serviceman or woman. I put it to him that we were excluding from Britain some of the bravest soldiers who had ever worn a British Army uniform. The smart looking civil servant intervened: 'I don't think the minister should answer that question.' I very much thought he *should* answer the question. I sensed the minster's unease. He repeated a whole series of platitudes about how valued the Gurkhas were, what a keen interest he had in the debate, that members of his team would be 'considering' the issue.

For me, this was a defining moment in the campaign. Here we were, sitting in a minister's office with the Gurkha issue attracting some media interest – indeed, I could see it running on BBC News 24 on a monitor at the back of the room. Yes, this was progress – we were talking to the right person. But you could almost feel the colossal inertia that the establishment can deploy when it simply doesn't want to move on an issue.

I left that meeting knowing that we had done no harm to our cause, but that we were still many miles from the massive momentum needed for us to have any chance of actually changing something.

We returned to Parliament for a briefing with Ming Campbell, now leader of the Lib Dems. Mr Campbell met us in the House of Commons with his colleague, Willie Rennie. He had a genuine interest in the situation and pledged to give us any support we needed, but like the rest of the day, though it felt useful it was not enough. Within hours, our meeting and our demonstration would fade, both from the ministerial and the public mind.

We needed to do something with more punch.

——————

Looking from the outside, campaigns are a bit like icebergs: most people just see the bit at the top. In any successful national campaign, people will see what is featured on the news and hits headlines; in reality, there is usually an enormous amount of energy and work that goes on unseen by most. It's understandable. After all, the majority of people live lives full to the brim of that chaotic mix of family, work and pleasure, combined with a myriad of other pressures. From a campaigning point of view, it's really important to realise this and then not lose track of that fact. There are so many campaigns where those at the centre, for whom that organisation and that cause probably dominates a huge part of their lives, end up so absorbed by the issue that they forget to look at it from the eyes of the 'man in the street'. Indeed, the art of campaigning lies, to a large extent, in shifting that balance. It's no good preaching to the converted or having intense debates amongst the campaign group – you have to get your message out to people and in such a way that they feel motivated to take action. For those of us at the centre of the Gurkha campaign, it was a case of constantly finding ways to get the issue to burst into the lives of others. If this isn't done, it means you can't develop that sense of momentum and excitement that is needed to feed the cycle of media interest and resultant political pressure. So often, I would find myself pondering – in the bath or when driving on long business trips to Barnsley or out to Newport in South Wales – the question of what to do next, what new angle to play.

Shaun Roberts had been my agent in the 2001 general election and been a constant source of advice throughout all my time with the Lib Dems. Shaun had cut his teeth on a whole host of local elections across Kent, particularly in the North Kent area around Sittingbourne. He was gifted. By that I mean that he had the innate skills needed for his role as political agent long before he ever went on any course. He had an instinct for knowing what messages to lead with and how to react to events as they inevitably unfold during any campaign, large or small.

I met Shaun completely by chance. It was 1998 and I had decided that I should finally head to Lib Dem HQ and go through the process of becoming officially sanctioned as someone who could stand for the party at a general election. At the time, these events were called Candidate Approval Days. I understand that they are now called Development Days. I imagine that part of the rationale behind this change was to avoid people who the party didn't think had made the grade feeling that they'd failed to meet 'approval' – methinks a case of political correctness gone mad.

On my Approval Day, I arrived at 4 Cowley Street, just around the corner from the Houses of Parliament. It's a distinguished building set in a beautiful Westminster road. The houses are quaint – neat Georgian window frames, hanging baskets, streetlamps that Charlie Chaplin could have swung around and, considering the location, a remarkable lack of traffic. They have always struck me as typical of genteel London.

This was a significant day for someone who at that point had done little more than help deliver leaflets in a couple of local elections. I had a strong desire to follow the path to fight a parliamentary seat as a Lib Dem and I knew that today would be vital. Fail the Approval Day and it would be pretty much a dead stop to my ambition. I confess to having been a little nervous about the whole venture.

I was not alone. A group were going through the process that day, giving it the feeling of a job interview. The nervous wannabes sat making small talk, waiting to go into the boardroom. I guess you could say that it was a bit like the apprentices going in to face Lord Sugar – well, maybe not quite that intimidating. Just by watching and listening you could spot the Mr Ambition, the Mrs Confident and the Mr Confused. I imagine you get a similar cross-section at any company's assessment days.

I could see then, and can still see now, why the party has to do this. I understand that it's the same in the other main political parties too. They're terrified that someone might end up being selected as a candidate who then makes a complete wally of themselves. Standing for elected office presents a whole series of potential pitfalls and dangers. It has been known for people to be selected as a candidate and then demonstrate a complete lack of understanding of the policies of the party they purport to represent. Worse, I have known cases where people have actually been elected at local level with pretty much an entirely different political philosophy from their party. Then there is the need for the candidate to be able to stand up and address a crowd or handle a press interview. There is a fear that someone might be selected who would turn to jelly when confronted by an opponent or journalist, lacking the skills and confidence to handle themselves. Hence, the various parties like to make sure their candidates have been taught to avoid at least some of the bear traps. Of course, there is a downside to all of this. The danger is that this approach to candidate approval and selection gets the

look and feel of a 'candidate factory'. It tends to miti-
gate against those with very powerful personalities or
quirks of character. Would some of our past political
greats have made it through a Candidate Approval
Day – Winston Churchill, David Lloyd George...?

But all that's by the by. The system was that you had
to have an Approval Day, and so I had no choice but
to go and seek approval. The day was a series of role
plays and other exercises, some individual, some team
based. One of the simpler tasks was to write a press
release – a document that people and organisations
send out to the media as a potential news story. In
my case, the scenario was that I, as a candidate in the
general election to become the MP for the mythical
seat of Blogshire, was to visit an old folks' home in the
constituency. Could I do this? I certainly could not.
I'd never written a press release in my life. I got into
a terrible muddle. It ended up being ten times longer
than it should have been. Worse, when I read the text
back, even I couldn't make any sense of it. I mention
this because as the Gurkha campaign was to grow and
grow I ended up having to write press releases not
just for the local papers and radio in Folkestone &
Hythe, but for the national and international media.
In the feedback session at the end of the dreaded day,
however, the judges duly ruled that my press release
was a catastrophic failure and I was 'sentenced' to a
training course on the subject.

The most amusing session came later in the day.
Politics at local and national level is littered with

examples of candidates who have been duly approved, selected in their local area and then found to have a skeleton in the cupboard that imperils their political future. The skeleton is usually discovered by the media or leaked out by an enemy, so in order to try and prevent this, the party conducts its own interviews to flush out any such worries. In my era this took the form of a one-to-one conversation with a member of the party's great and good in a side office. The rules were explained. One was to spill all and, in return, any revelations would be treated in MI5/MI6 style secrecy. The intention was to identify any indiscretions – sexual, financial or other – that could lead to embarrassment. Once the beans had been spilt, an assessment could be made as to whether the 'sin' was cardinal and you couldn't stand, or 'manageable' and the party would get itself and you, the candidate, through the fall-out should the matter become a revelation.

What a dilemma for me. I had nothing to confess. 'Oh My God,' I thought, 'they'll think I'm so boring.' It crossed my mind that I should try and invent something that might avoid the label of 'dull', whilst not incurring a look that clearly said 'That's appalling' from my inquisitor. I'd never taken a single illicit drug of any kind. I'd only ever had one puff of a normal cigarette before it made me sick – and that was at school. As for any sexual scandal – I'd never been that lucky. Mercifully, after that temporary madness, I sensibly opted for unexciting honesty. My inquisitor, who had obviously been on a 'stare 'em in the eye' course, calmly said, 'Oh, that's good.' Secretly, I reckon he was saying, 'Yep. He's boring.'

I left my day unsure of how it had gone. When they came, the results confirmed my fears. I was to attend a course on how to write press releases – but there was more. They were concerned by my lack of campaigning experience. I was told that before they would approve me to stand for Parliament, I had to fight a local campaign somewhere for the party so that I could 'learn the ropes'.

On the Approval Day I had met Elvie Lowe, who was there so that she could stand to be the MP for Sittingbourne & Sheppey. We got on well and I had offered her a lift home since we lived in the same area. Elvie had mentioned that they were in need of candidates to fight several wards in the area, including Iwade & Lower Halstow. I had thought little of it at the time, but when my judgment came through the conversation returned to me. After due process I was selected as the local candidate for Iwade & Lower Halstow. And thus, I met Shaun. He was acting as agent for Elvie and all the other Lib Dems in the area, fitting this political work around his full-time job with ICL maintaining the computer systems at various important railway stations in London. Shaun arrived at my home in Hartlip, just outside Sittingbourne, and gave me a box containing maps and a list of local electors. He explained that the seat hadn't seen any Lib Dem activity for years, it was pretty hopeless, that everyone else would be working in more winnable wards, that I needed to work hard, to knock on every door, and he would see me later. This was my true introduction to Lib Dem grassroots campaigning. Shaun and I were to become great friends and work together on many successful local election campaigns.

And in February 2008 it was Shaun who came up with the brilliant idea that a selection of retired Gurkhas should hand back their medals as a sign of protest against the continuing exclusion of pre-1997 retirees. Returning medals had been prominent in some of the key anti-Vietnam War protests in America, but how would it go down here in the UK with both the Gurkhas and the public?

Military people value their medals. They really mean something to the wearer. For the Gurkhas, I suspect that this feeling is heightened as they are denied so many other things. Even back in Nepal, where we as a country condemn thousands of retired Gurkhas to live in poverty and in conditions that we would find totally unacceptable, medals are still worn with an immense amount of pride. From a campaigning and publicity point of view, this idea had attractions. It would almost certainly attract media interest. More than that, if we did this in Westminster, I felt sure that it could be used to apply a degree of political pressure. I needed to see and assess how the Gurkhas themselves would feel about this.

I consulted with Gopal Giri, one of the original four Gurkhas who had set me on this path, and his friend Dhan Gurung, the first retired Gurkha ever to be elected to a UK local council, and they in turn asked various members of their community. The Gurkhas gave the idea the green light and we started to plan.

I took Madan Gurung to meet with Charles Kennedy and Ming Campbell's successor, Nick Clegg, in his House of Commons office a few days before the actual 'ceremony' for handing back the medals. The Lib Dem Leader's office was up a ridiculously narrow staircase. I had been in this office before, in the early days of the campaign when the party was under Kennedy's stewardship. We waited on the landing area outside, like the staircase its dimensions making it impossible to not be in the way, until the staff and assistants kindly showed us through.

I briefed Nick on the plan. We needed to secure the maximum publicity possible on the day. Therefore, we asked if Nick would use one of his questions at Prime Minister's Questions to highlight the issue. We talked through what that question could be, how it should be framed and whether we could or should use the medals as a 'prop' during PMQs. In my mind's eye, I wanted Nick to have a box of medals and actually attempt to give these to Gordon Brown across the floor of the House. I suspect that Nick liked the edginess of this, but both he and his staff were very aware of the protocol and traditions of the House – the use of props and 'stunts' such as this were definitely not allowed. I knew this too, but such was my strength of feeling that I hoped he would be persuaded on this point and that he might end up being banned from the House. I imagine that there would have been huge implications had this indeed happened. However, from the perspective of our campaign it would have been gold dust.

In the end, the best degree of 'theatre' that I could persuade Nick and his team to go with involved Madan's medal. Nick would take it with him and hold it up during one of his questions to the Prime Minister.

The day came. The Gurkhas had organised a small fleet of coaches to collect them from the various areas of the retired Gurkha community. I travelled up by car, listening to BBC Radio Kent on the way into London. Our story was only about the third or fourth item on their news programme. My car passed one of the Gurkha coaches on the A2 as we were approaching the Blackwall Tunnel. There they were, turned out in their classic civilian uniform. Through the gloom of the winter morning I could see several of them resting their heads against the coach windows having rubbed a patch of visibility through the condensation. For some reason, I felt incredibly depressed at that point. It came on suddenly. Had I marched them up a hill to a fight they couldn't win? Was I deluding them and myself? Were we going to get to a point where we were always stuck at number three on the regional radio news, always fighting and struggling but never getting anywhere? And how much longer could I keep going before I had to tell them that I had simply run out of campaigning ideas? It's easy to talk of 'never giving up' when you are not the one taking the ups and downs and facing the frustrations. When you're in the middle of it, coping with all the stresses and strains of 'normal life' with everything else on top, it gets wearing. This felt like the campaign equivalent of battle fatigue. Within minutes, the phone rang and my mind was jolted out of that lonely place to deal with the here and now.

We gathered in Old Palace Yard. The plan was that Nick would come out with his defence team and receive the medals from the assembled Gurkha throng. We had gone through the chore of getting all the necessary police permissions to demonstrate and even had consent to use the loud hailer. The press turned up in reasonable numbers. Some of the photographers wanted the event to be choreographed with the palace of Westminster in the background. For this to be achieved, I had to try and persuade the crowd of Gurkhas, now swelled to perhaps four or five hundred, to change location. It all got very chaotic, to say the least. Throughout the campaign, I was to learn that Gurkhas in the army are well drilled, but controlling groups of retired Gurkhas in civvy life is worse than herding cats.

Fifty retired Gurkhas had agreed to hand in their medals. The plan was that these would be placed in a box and presented to Nick Clegg, who would then attempt to arrange a way of handing these over to Gordon Brown, the Prime Minister. Nick arrived and the waiting Gurkhas were delighted. In their desire to see him and to thank him, the crowd surged forward and it all became a bit of a crush. But when the moment came for the medals to be handed back, suddenly the atmosphere changed profoundly. For the most part, these were long service and good conduct medals. For a Gurkha to hand over this potent symbol of the very thing they pride themselves on so much – their service and their loyalty – was a wrench. It was emotional and upsetting. Crying is not something normally associated with the Gurkhas, yet there were tears of anger, hurt and deep, deep frustration. As the medals tumbled into the small cardboard chest that they had picked as a receptacle, a few made short speeches. Some quoted their name, rank and number. Others mentioned their family history of service with the brigade. Many stated the years of service given. Gopal Giri surrendered more than just his long service and good conduct medal. He held up his deeply treasured MBE before placing that too into the box.

There is always a concern that events such as this could be seen as and portrayed by a cynical media as mere stunts designed purely to attract attention. The deep emotional reaction from the Gurkhas showed that this was so much more than that. The ceremony had served its purpose. It had showed the press and the watching world just how profoundly the situation was affecting the Gurkhas.

Nick Clegg duly challenged Gordon Brown in the chamber with Madan's medal held high. This brought a well-written and much rehearsed response from the Prime Minister, who reiterated the same old words about 1997 and Hong Kong, but it may have been telling that his voice took on the tone of an angry wounded bear when he gave his reply.

From the campaign's point of view, we had secured the media's interest and had forced the issue, however briefly, into the political arena. For the moment, job done.

Nick's office made several attempts to arrange for Nick to hand the box of medals over to Number 10 but each of these came to nothing. Some weeks passed – still no progress. This simply could not go on.

I called Downing Street and asked for a slot to hand in a petition at the door, as we had done on many previous occasions. This time, however, it wouldn't be a petition that we would try and hand in – it would be the medals.

There are all sorts of rules and protocols surrounding submitting petitions at the door of Number 10. So how would they handle this unusual offering? Would they accept the medals or reject them? What would we do if the commissionaire refused them – take them back, or just leave them there?

Yet again we made arrangements for a group of retired Gurkhas to meet up with me in Old Palace Yard. This time, on 25 June 2008, it was a much smaller event. Inspired by the heroism of our small band and by one member in particular, Tul Bahadur Pun VC, we printed out thirteen large white placards, each simply displaying an image of a Victoria Cross to symbolise the thirteen VCs won by Gurkha soldiers (their British Officers had won another thirteen), and marshalled them into a dignified line. There would be no box this time – the Gurkhas and I had decided that to both display and protect the medals, they should be attached to a large wooden board of about three feet by two feet in size covered with the type of green fabric that lines snooker tables.

At the appointed hour, Nick Clegg emerged from Parliament and made his way to meet us. Our small group set off on the short walk from Old Palace Yard, skirting around Parliament Square and proceeding up Whitehall to the gates of Downing Street. We must have been a bit of an odd collection. Tul was in his wheelchair; Dhan Gurung was carrying the medal board; Nick and I and the rest of the party probably looked like a group of tourists as we wove our way through the dense pedestrian throng.

We entered Downing Street and went through all the normal security checks. Nick and I had become slightly separated from the others and, while we waited for them to catch up, I shared my fears with him. I had asked for clearance to present a letter or petition to the door, and that would be what Downing Street were expecting; instead, they would find a medal board, loaded with long service and good conduct medals and an MBE. 'Nick,' I said, 'How do you want to play this if they refuse to accept them?'

I was all for just putting the medals down on the steps and daring the police or someone from inside Downing Street to move them. Nick was concerned that this might look disrespectful and cheapen our cause. He seemed extremely anxious about how best to go about this. We tossed ideas around for quite a few minutes. This, I realised, was where my campaigning heart clashed with his political head, so I let him know that I understood that this could affect his reputation as a senior politician and told him he must act as he saw fit. That said, I was absolutely determined that those medals would be seen going through that door. The point had to be made. It would be unbelievably rude of the government to refuse these medals and unbelievably silly from a political perspective to appear dismissive of the protest. I was convinced that if the police had to pick up those medals and deal with them, the government would be giving us a major opportunity to further pile on the pressure.

We assembled as a party on the steps of 10 Downing Street and knocked on the lacquered black door's great brass knocker. The door swung open and the commissionaire filled the frame. Without blinking an eye, he reached out to accept our precious board of medals and we posed for a photograph – utterly shell-shocked. Against all odds, the medals had made it into Number 10.

The story ran well for us, hitting the regional BBC and several of the broadsheet newspapers. John Ingham at the *Daily Express*, as ever, did the Gurkhas proud, as did the *Daily Mail*. But I sometimes ask myself if those readers and viewers ever wondered what happened to the medals. They were put into storage – a military base in Stafford, I understand. Some weeks after the ultimate campaign victory, I suggested to the Downing Street communications unit that the government could secure some very swift and positive PR by arranging to give the medals back to those retired Gurkhas who had 'sacrificed' them. But to no avail. They continued to lie in storage. And there they are still.

TUL BAHADUR PUN VC

Tul Bahadur Pun VC held a special place in the campaign, gracing nearly every one of our events.

Tul Bahadur Pun won his Victoria Cross out in the Far East during the Second World War. In an act of great heroism, Pun picked up a heavy machine gun and ran directly at a heavily defended Japanese position, over thick mud and difficult terrain and through a hail of bullets. It should have meant certain death. Without his bravery, so many more men would have died.

As Pun had retired from the army decades before the 1997 cut-off date, he too was denied access to Britain because he 'did not have a close enough tie to the country'. This was eventually overcome when the then immigration minister, Liam Byrne, made an 'exception' to allow him to stay.

There was to be further controversy surrounding Pun. There were several issues surrounding securing him medical treatment at a west London hospital. Apparently, he was challenged by a rather aggressive member of staff who doubted his entitlement to be in Britain. During the questioning, the member of staff asked: 'What's this VC bit after your name ... what does that mean?'

FIVE

FAME

———•———

Who, I wondered suspiciously, was the man in the smart dark suit? Was he Ministry of Defence? Was he from the police? What exactly was his interest in the Gurkha issue? These were the thoughts that went through my mind when I first met David Enright. It turned out that I couldn't be any further from the truth. David was one of the team at Howe & Co. – a firm of human rights and immigration lawyers based in west London. Just like me, they had developed a very strong interest indeed in retired Gurkha affairs and the issue of settlement in the UK and, hearing of one of our many Gurkha protests in Westminster, David had resolved to come along to see what was happening.

Quite separately from anything that I was doing, Howe & Co. had started to take on individual Gurkha cases and contest them in the asylum and immigration courts. Their top team consisted of Martin and David Howe, Kieran O'Rourke and the aforementioned David Enright. All were passionate advocates for their retired Gurkha clients, becoming de facto experts in law relating to Gurkha issues. They even had an office in Nepal.

It is no exaggeration to say that Howe & Co.'s involvement was absolutely crucial to the success of the Gurkha Justice campaign. We started to work together closely, exchanging ideas and sparking off each other. The team's legal work on its own was of the utmost importance. However, their contribution extended far beyond that – the lawyers were woven into the very fabric of the overall campaign.

I recall one particular conversation with Kieran over a drink in St Stephen's tavern, which sits in the shadow of Big Ben on the edge of Parliament Square. Kieran was explaining to one of my Lib Dem colleagues how the issue had affected him. Quite naturally, and without any disruption to the flow of the conversation, Kieran started to cry. Tears were streaming down his face. Such was the intensity of his belief that retired Gurkhas should be respected under the law.

With the courts flooded with the individual cases, Howe & Co. had filed for a judicial review of Gurkha settlement rights. Kieran and I talked long and often about how best we could choreograph the events surrounding the review. What media interest could we attract?

What would we need to do to rouse interest? I pressed Nick Clegg's office in the hope that he might attend the hearing at some point. Various groups of Gurkhas were marshalled to provide a phalanx of supporters outside the court for the duration of proceedings.

We decided that the day before the start of the court case would be crucial. Our plan was to hand in yet another petition to Downing Street combined with a march to the Gurkha memorial outside the MoD.

Having taken some time out from local politics, I had decided to have another go at being an MP. I had strong connections with Maidstone & The Weald constituency, the seat occupied for many years by Ann Widdecombe. Hearing that she was to be retiring, I put myself forward for selection as the Lib Dem candidate and was duly selected.

There seemed to be a lot of sense in raising the Gurkha issue in my new constituency – it was a cause for which I was actively campaigning and I felt that my views might strike a chord with many people across the area. I resolved to go out into one of the more rural areas, the so-called 'capital of the Weald', Cranbrook, and collect signatures there. I've always really liked Cranbrook. It's the sort of town that the BBC could make a 1950s drama in without changing much at all. The shops are interesting and a bit quirky, there are 'proper' tea shops with real pots of tea and chequered table cloths, and people seem to have a few extra minutes to pass the time of day. It's definitely my kind of town.

Little did I know it, but the decision to go to Cranbrook on that particular day, at that particular time would have a profound – perhaps the most profound – impact on our campaign. If ever there was to be an example of how major events pivot on the smallest occurrences, this would surely be it. The tidal wave of media coverage that was to follow may well never have happened had I not chosen splendid, charming Cranbrook as the place to try my luck.

The petition gathered a lot of interest as we stood on the corner outside Vestry Hall. Cranbrook has a political reputation of being 'deep blue' and a few people, a little rudely, questioned my motives for helping this particular cause. But it was only a very few, and I had become used to actual abuse rather than cynicism from hardened true blue activists that I had fought so hard against in Folkestone & Hythe. There, they would allege that everything I had ever done for the Gurkhas was simply 'electioneering'. They would maintain this even though, for long periods, I kept fighting for the issue when I wasn't in the running for any seat or elected office. Only the eventual Gurkha Justice victory softened their slightly embittered thoughts. A fair degree of cynicism is probably healthy in a democracy, but it can be tiresome when it overshadows everything that people try to do. So it was a relief that Cranbrook was generally so much more supportive.

Sometime just before noon that day a lady came to sign the petition and made the passing remark that was to be one of the most crucial moments of the campaign. 'You're doing well with this, but you need someone famous to help you – why don't you get in touch with Joanna Lumley?' she said, before going off about her business. I heard her, but thought little of it.

Later that evening, sat at home in the conservatory that serves as our dining room, her comment came back to me. The thought was like a little worm in your brain, burrowed deep and impossible to get out. I've always believed that sometimes you just have to do something, regardless of whether it is odd or unconventional – like trying to contact Joanna Lumley from your dining room. By doing the 'difficult' thing, the thing that most people would think so unlikely as to be not worth trying, you sometimes unleash a series of events that really make magic happen.

But where and how to start trying to track down the *Absolutely Fabulous* star? I suddenly recalled Kieran mentioning that Joanna had expressed support in an earlier campaign to get Tul Bahadur Pun VC into Britain. I wasn't involved in this particular battle, but the Howe & Co. team were. Joanna had been active on one of the military websites and Kieran had suggested to her that she might be able to write supportive letters to the press about Tul Bahadur Pun. This she did.

I emailed Kieran who sent over an email address that he thought might get through to someone who possibly knew Joanna. In case this didn't work, I searched for Joanna Lumley on Google and ended up with all sorts of curious information about celebrities.

I had no idea just how prurient people are, wanting to know all the ins and outs of which celebrity is doing what with which other – there was a whole plethora of fan-type websites. In the end, I sent out a whole series of emails to one and all and, to be frank, wasn't hopeful that I'd get a response. Frustrated and feeling slightly that this whole venture was a fairly hopeless task, I even tried directory enquiries.

'Hello – what name please?'

'Lumley'

'Initial?'

'J.'

'What address?'

I had to guess a little here, 'London – I think – but it might be Kent.'

Well, you guessed it – I couldn't get her number by that route.

Some weeks later, I was travelling back from Yorkshire when I realised that I hadn't checked the answer phone on my 'in-car' mobile yet that day. So after my customary Little Chef Olympic Breakfast stop, I decided I'd check my messages before setting off down the long, dark A1.

The first three were routine: one from work and the other two related to my position on the local council in Cheriton, Folkestone. The first of these was about rats in local allotments and sounded pretty pressing; the second was about a person with a benefit claim query – such is the drama of political life at local level. However, the message that came next was...

'Hello, it's Joanna, please call me on...'

I recall being a bit annoyed. 'Joanna' didn't give me a clue what I would be calling her about – would it be the rats? Or perhaps another benefit claim? Years of experience trying to help local people with issues or problems had taught me how useful it could be to have a heads up on a message.

I called the number and after a few seconds real-ised that this had absolutely nothing to do with my duties as a local councillor. This was Joanna – as in Lumley. As in the Joanna Lumley I had seen on Michael Parkinson's show so many years before. As in the Joanna Lumley I knew had starred in something called *Absolutely Fabulous*. I had watched part of an episode of the show and, to be honest, it left me cold. I just didn't get it at all. I was later to confess this to Joanna, who graciously shared the fact that neither did her father. I felt a little better – not just me then.

I laid out the issue behind the campaign, our current situation and the up-coming court case. Joanna asked a number of questions: what or who was preventing the retired Gurkhas from applying to settle in Britain? What was the significance of the 1997 date? It was during this conversation that Joanna told me about her connection to Tul Bahadur Pun VC, explaining that this particular Gurkha had served with her father. The conversation was short and focused. Finally, she said that she would help.

I sped off down the A1 back to Kent, my mind work-ing overtime on what this might mean. How much impact would this have? Would this transform our media coverage? Would it ever.

The weeks passed and preparations for the High Court demonstrations developed apace. The plan was to gather once again in Old Palace Yard and then march the now familiar path past Parliament Square and then up Whitehall. A small delegation would then enter Downing Street and hand the latest petition in at the door of Number 10. Following that, the march would resume and continue on to the Gurkha memorial located right outside the Ministry of Defence main entrance. This memorial is inscribed with a quote from Sir Ralph Turner: 'Bravest of the brave, most generous of the generous, never had country more faithful friends than you.' It always struck me as odd that this memorial, with these eloquent and moving words, was located outside the very building that seemingly housed an almost implacable opposition to our cause.

On the day, the Gurkhas laid a wreath and a few simple speeches were made. Tomorrow would be High Court day and Joanna would enter the battle.

SIX

HIGH COURT START DAY
17/9/2008

———————•◆•———————

After decades of watching the main news bulletins on any of the major TV channels I felt strangely familiar with the High Court in the Strand. So many times I'd seen it appear as the backdrop for some high profile case or other that had made the news. There it would stand, almost like a great Gothic cathedral. The leading solicitor of the winning team would emerge, usually flanked by the plaintiff, and read the victory statement to the cheers of gleeful supporters. It seemed to me that the end of any significant legal battle in the nation's history was played out on the steps of this imposing building. Would our legal battle end in similar vein – or would we leave defeated?

GURKHA

We went to the High Court on the 17 September 2008. What the lawyers had been pushing for, and had now achieved, was a judicial review of the whole system of law relating to Gurkha immigration, high-lighting in particular the 1997 cut-off date. The case was to be heard by Justice Blake. His judgment was expected to be announced some time towards the end of the month.

That first day started early. *BBC Breakfast* had requested that Joanna go on the sofa to be inter-viewed by presenters Sian Williams and Bill Turnbull, together with one of the band of retired Gurkhas who could bear testament to the hurt and anguish felt by himself and thousands of his colleagues. I knew that exposure on a show such as this was crucial: it reached literally hundreds of thousands of people and it was difficult to imagine any other means of campaigning that could get our message out in such an effective way. Somehow, we had to make that happen – no matter how early we had to get out of bed. Lynne and I got up at some ungodly hour of the night in Folkestone and drove up a deserted M20 to the little house in Maidstone, 133 Bower Street, that I was renting from a friend and in which I had insisted Madan Kunar Gurung and his wife Meena make their home. Quite simply, they had nowhere else to go. When I first met them, they were living on the kindness of others in a small bedsit in Tonbridge.

Once we had arrived in Maidstone, the wonder-fully slick logistics of the BBC swung into action and they laid on a car to collect us all from Bower Street at 5.30 a.m. We were driven through the silent streets of London and arrived at Shepherd's Bush at 6.30 a.m.

We found ourselves at the BBC Television Centre well in advance of our assigned slot. I couldn't help but enjoy the experience of being in this famous building. For years of my childhood, I, and I suspect a lot of people of a similar age to me, watched John Noakes and Valerie Singleton battle with 'get down Shep' in the *Blue Peter* garden. So often, I've encountered buildings and people in real life after seeing them on TV and been a bit unimpressed. TV seems to make me think that things are big and imposing and on many occasions I've found the reality to be a lot less so. However, I found booking in at security and going to the stage door quite an adventure – perhaps it was the little boy in me. I almost felt I should have had some milk bottle tops ready for the next *Blue Peter* Appeal.

Having been met at reception, we were escorted through a myriad of curved corridors in the heart of the building known to many as 'The Doughnut'. It was worse than the *Crystal Maze*. Eventually, our small party arrived at the green room for *BBC Breakfast*, which was slightly larger than a wardrobe but had the nectar of tea and Danish pastries to help our bodies get over that 'you've been up since 3 a.m. feeling'. I paced around outside the room going over everything that we needed to make happen that day. And it was then that I met Joanna for the first time.

She emerged from behind the curve of the corridor

wearing soft and silent shoes. She was much smaller than I had imagined and, for a moment, didn't actually look anything like Joanna Lumley. Lots of the BBC staff started to fuss around her. I walked over, introduced myself, shook her hand and thanked her for taking on the campaign. Anxious not to cause offence by underestimating her knowledge, I asked if it would be useful to run through the background and the key points. As would happen so many times in the following tumultuous months, she said, 'Peter, that would be wonderful... Please do.' I quietly spoke into Joanna's ear and gave her a comprehensive run-down of the situation, including the complexity of the 1997 cut-off, what it meant, how it was hurting people like Madan and what we were calling on the government to do. She asked no questions.

As my whispered briefing came to an end, the floor manager appeared and ushered Joanna and Madan in. For a brief moment, Lynne, Meena and I saw the studio through the open door. I've done a fair bit of TV work since the Gurkha campaign. On that day, I experienced something that always strikes me now when I enter a TV studio – I call it 'liquid silence'. The quietness in these studios is so intense it almost feels fluid – you can literally feel the 'hush' enveloping you. Bizarrely, it's like that even when someone is speaking, which feels vaguely off-putting. Joanna and Madan disappeared inside and we gathered around the TV set in the green room to watch the interview unfold. Lynne and I had our hearts in our mouths as

Sian asked Madan to describe the injustices he had faced. We'd often worried about the enormous stress that fighting this campaign would place on the likes of Madan. Here was a gentle man, worn down by years of struggling to stay in Britain against the odds, with very little money, with great uncertainly about his housing and his entire future – and what did we ask him to do? Go live on TV in front of millions of people. Madan spoke with a slightly faltering voice and trembling emotion. Somehow, this made his contribution all the more compelling. Joanna looked on, radiating support for him. When it came, her contribution was measured, perfect in its accuracy, and I could already feel that she was making a strong link with the public at large. By now, I had worked out what made a powerful TV image, and this was it.

Once filming was over, Lynne and Joanna discovered a shared joy. Smoking. There followed a swift exit to the open-air part of the Doughnut – the inner courtyard – and much flapping of handbags and frantic rustling in their darkest depths to locate the toxin sticks.

As we stood outside, Joanna was able to do some radio interviews from my mobile phone. Most notably, she did BBC Radio Kent. Radio Kent is living testament to the power of local radio in community life. Kent is home to most of the currently serving Gurkhas and the radio station was anxious to cover the story from its humble origins all the way through to the point when we would win against all the odds.

They reported on our progress in good times and bad. For that reason, I always made sure that on any 'big day' in the campaign I found the time for Joanna and the other key players to talk to them. To be honest, I sometimes got the impression that they were thrilled to get a national star on their airwaves – but they never let on.

The BBC had kindly offered to supply transport for Joanna from the BBC Television Centre to the High Court. Looking back on it, even this minor logistical detail felt fraught with potential problems at the time. Here we were, a group of people who did not actually know each other trying to negotiate a complex and unfamiliar scenario. Joanna had mentioned in an earlier email that the BBC was going to arrange this car for her. Great, I thought, but what about us? Unsure of the etiquette, I vaguely suggested that perhaps Lynne, Madan, Meena and I might ride with her. Graciously, she agreed. Despite my fears, so much was to come together seamlessly in this rush of fast-moving events.

Kieran and I had agreed that Joanna's arrival needed to be choreographed carefully in order to achieve the greatest impact possible. Kieran was already in position outside the High Court with a multitude of retired Gurkhas and their families, and he and I now exchanged phone calls back and forth as the car began to weave through south-west London, using our mobiles like walkie-talkies.

Kieran reported that there was a strong showing of media waiting for us on the steps of the High Court – I was soon to learn just how strong 'strong' was. I don't know where it came from, but early in the campaign I somehow developed an awareness that pretty much every step in a campaign such as ours had to be managed and controlled. Even apparently simple things like getting out of the car and into the building took careful coordination. Faced with the crush of journalists, Joanna adopted what became known to me as her 'serene' mode. She was to do this many times in the campaign, particularly during the manic visit to Nepal. She sat how you would imagine a model would sit – composed, upright, with a look that if you didn't know better might suggest she was oblivious to what was going on around her. And at this early stage, I really didn't know any better, hampered as I was by not yet knowing Joanna very well. What I really wanted to say was: 'Right, when we stop, don't move, don't open the door, wait until I get out and open the door for you – until we have worked out how we deal with this mêlée.' But instead I had to prefix each of my commands with 'Do you think it would be a good idea if...?' I couldn't just dictate to someone I didn't know.

As we drove down the Strand and passed St Clement Danes church, we asked the BBC driver to slow a little in response to a request from Kieran, who was frantically trying to get the retired Gurkhas and the media sorted into some kind of order.

Eventually, our blue people carrier slowed to a halt directly outside the court and suddenly everything in the car went dark. Literally, black. An eclipse of the sun?

No – a greeting from the press pack. There were bodies and cameras pressed against every window. I had to push with all my weight against the back passenger door so that I could force a way out – and once out of the car, I ended up squashed back against it. Please, whenever you see such an arrival by a celebrity or politician on the TV, spare a thought for the guy in the suit – on this occasion, me – who just gets crushed. I managed to pull Joanna's door open and used my body and arms to shield her from the enormous mob of photographers. I'm not sure what the collective noun is for press photographers – if there is one it must surely be the same as that used for carnivores who rip their prey to pieces. Joanna emerged, quite correctly, in serene mode. By now, one of the Gurkhas most active in the campaign and one of the original four to visit me at home, Bhim, had realised our plight and come to the rescue. Bhim has the useful characteristic of being as broad as he is long. He and Kieran formed a human shield, with arms interlocked, and walked backwards up the courthouse steps, clearing the way for Joanna.

The journey up those steps took some time – each step a small victory. Finally, we were halted by the row of retired Gurkhas waiting at that first level area just before the main entrance. Two of the Gurkhas were in their wheelchairs. Joanna approached them.

The two men were Tul Bahadur Pun VC and Lechiman Gurung VC. It is unlikely that you could ever conceive of two braver souls than these. Joanna had told me during one of our earliest conversations that she would very much like to meet Pun, who had served with her father in the Far East in appalling conditions, against appalling odds. Joanna's father, Major James Lumley, had been a Chindit, fighting in the jungle as what could, in modern terms, be viewed as a mixture of commando and Special Forces: unconventional and exceptionally driven to succeed and survive. Joanna had been told of Pun's immense courage by her father, who had given his daughter a photograph of the man who had saved his life whilst serving him; but the two had never met.

So here it was – that first meeting – on the steps of the High Court, in the full glare and blaze of the world's media. Joanna had bought Pun a small gift. As she stooped to give it to him, he looked up, raised his hand to the side of her face and, through his interpreter, said: 'I remember your father. It is as if you are my daughter.' Suddenly, through the cacophony and the chaos on the steps of the court, through the complexity and frustrations of fighting a national campaign against a determined government, the raw compelling emotion of this whole crusade was crystallised in that moment. It rooted me to the floor. Just for a split second, Joanna's serenity gave way to vulnerability. She welled up. The exchange was caught supremely by one of the press photographers – Joanna wiping away a tear with one hand, the other on Pun's shoulder. I keep a copy of that photograph to this day. That one image captured the very essence of the feeling behind the tens of thousands of letters and petition signatures that were pouring into our home. There had never been any possibility of me turning my back on this cause, but if there ever had have been, I know that moment would have quashed the doubt in an instant.

Through a barrage of media questions and camera flashes we escorted Joanna up the remaining steps into the court.

SEVEN

HIGH COURT END DAY
30/9/2008

———•◄———

The High Court case lasted a couple of weeks. The team from Howe & Co. worked tirelessly with Counsel Ed Fitzgerald QC, Mark O'Connor and Mark Henderson, and after the hearings in court the judge retired to consider his ruling. During this period the campaign went into a curious state of suspended animation. So much would hang on the outcome of this hearing. I was rapidly trying to learn from the Howe & Co. team what the various possibilities would mean. I imagine that many people would have held the same view as me: I naively assumed that if we won the case – that is, if the judge ruled that excluding pre-1997 retired Gurkhas was unlawful – that the government would have to do what the rest of us do when we have transgressed: change its behaviour and accept the ruling of the court. Simple. But to my amazement, it wouldn't work like that. Even if the court were to rule that the treatment of these pre-1997 warriors was unlawful, it could not order the government to let them enter and stay in Britain. Instead, the court would set out the grounds for why this treatment was unlawful, then order the government to come back with a new set of guidelines. This subtle difference was to have a profound influence on events in the coming months.

During the tense days of waiting the legal ruling, Joanna and I discussed possible outcomes and what each might mean for the overall campaign. Joanna had actually been in court on the first day of the hearing. She described to me how the whole tone of the proceedings had left her with a heavy heart, but we both readily acknowledged that we were not experienced or learned enough in the law to form a reliable view. As the day of the judgment drew closer, my telephone calls to and from Howe & Co. increased in frequency and expectation.

Kieran had explained to me that the Howe & Co. team would receive notice of the ruling before it was made public. He set out for me just how strict the rules were surrounding who could have access to this early notification. Pretty much, it sounded like if they told Joanna and me before the information was made public, we would all be accused of contempt of court and sent to the Tower of London to be beheaded.

Kieran called me. I was at work. He couldn't possibly reveal what was in the ruling, but Kieran, being Kieran, didn't actually need to tell me that the judge had found in our favour – though Kieran is a highly educated, sincere, mature human being, he doesn't hide his emotions at all well, and I could tell that he and the other lawyers were beside themselves with excitement and joy. In the whole conversation I don't think I got out more than a 'That's interesting', such was the Gatling gun delivery from Kieran. The call ended and I was elated. I felt that stab of adrenalin in the base of my back that you get when somehow your whole body and mind reacts to startling news. To win this case would be a boost of incalculable proportions to the campaign. I took a few minutes to calm down and drink in the emotion of the moment. I told myself that I couldn't be sure that I'd interpreted Kieran's voice correctly ... but he did sound excited...

And now to tell Joanna. I called and left a message on her answer phone – she had an amusing way of saying 'beep', as in '...leave your message after the beep'. To this day, I cannot hear the word 'beep' without smiling at this idiosyncrasy.

She called back almost immediately. I said, 'I think we've won.' There was a short pause and then she simply said, 'Peter ... Oh, that would be wonderful ... Oh Peter, that would be wonderful' in that very Joannaesque way. The adrenalin came back and I sensed that she too knew this was truly a moment to savour. I heard her gasp slightly over the phone line.

If this victory was indeed confirmed, it would mean that the campaign was right on track. Joanna and I resolved that we needed a big show on the steps of the High Court to mark the formal announcement of the ruling. I had worked out that the legal victory in the High Court could actually become a bit of a bear trap in terms of the overall campaign. The image of delighted Gurkhas emerging from court with Joanna in full 'Ayo Gurkhali' mode might persuade many members of the public that no more effort was required, that victory had been secured and that the Gurkhas could come to Britain. But this legal 'victory' was only a stepping stone. It wouldn't be enough to just celebrate this victory in the High Court. We would need to use it as the launch pad for the next phase of the campaign – pressuring the government to actually change the immigration laws in our favour and let the pre-1997 retirees settle here.

The ruling was to be delivered on Tuesday 30 September. By now, Kieran and Martin had been able to explain more fully that, though we had won, the judge would rule that the government must go away and devise a new policy for pre-1997 Gurkhas. The judge had even set out a timescale for the government's response: it was to come back with new proposals within three months. It was absolutely necessary, therefore, that the Gurkha Justice group start campaigning immediately to make sure that the government didn't try and rewrite the policy in a minimalist way – doing just enough to satisfy the judge, but still discriminating against the Gurkhas and keeping the majority out.

The weekend before the ruling, I'd had the honour of a visit to my home by the then Nepali Foreign Minister, Sujata Koirala, who was a relative of Dhan Gurung, by now a close friend back in Folkestone. To honour her visit Lynne and I hosted a small reception. Another guest at the 'do' was one of my fellow Liberal Democrat campaigners and councillors, Tim Prater. Tim was responsible for building websites for literally hundreds of local Liberal Democrat associations.

I took advantage of a lull in the party to go into a huddle with Tim. I explained that if we should win the High Court case, which by now I knew we had but couldn't tell him, we would need to launch the next campaign phase immediately.

I asked Tim to work a miracle – we needed a website up and running within days so that Joanna could announce it on those court steps. And work a miracle he did. A very simple website (www.gurkhajustice. org.uk) was put together at breakneck speed. I knew that we would have to fund this web development, but right now time was of the essence. Tim took it on trust that somehow we'd find the funding. In fact, Joanna and I had agreed by phone that we would jointly fund this if another source was not forthcoming.

Our concern over funding the development of the website was to be short-lived. I was working late into the night, as was normal during this frenetic stage, since there were literally hundreds upon hundreds of letters and emails to sift through and collate. The job of organising paper correspondence was to grow to the point that Lynne and I needed the help of Maggie Barrett-Sheldrake, a long-time friend and fellow Lib Dem. However, I was still looking after the bulk of the email traffic.

An email came in. It was very short and to the point, saying something along the lines of 'My name is Jack. I'm out in the Bahamas. I want to help.' I consulted with Joanna. Save for the reference to the Bahamas, it was unremarkable, no different from the hundreds of others. Yet, Joanna confirmed, this was Sir Jack Haywood, famed for his entrepreneurial spirit, his love of all things British, for his support of Wolverhampton Wanderers and for the dozens of projects that he had helped across the years. Rachael Heyhoe-Flint helped Sir Jack run his affairs in the UK. Both Rachael and Sir Jack were steadfast and generous in their support for our fight.

We nervously asked if Sir Jack would consider donating about £4,000 to help us take the fight to the internet in a really serious way. He responded by email: 'I'm sending you £20,000. Don't lose. If you don't use all the money, give the rest to the Gurkha Welfare Trust.' Joanna was custodian of the money. As it transpired, people were extremely generous, helping to fund the campaign by sending small donations and buying Gurkha Justice memorabilia. Added to that, we all covered our own expenses, so the need for money was kept to an absolute minimum. A very large proportion of Sir Jack's money, therefore, did indeed end up being handed over to the GWT.

The website, with its online petition, played a crucial role in the ongoing campaign. Tim, its designer and creator, urged us to use YouTube videos to make the site fresh and engaging, and Joanna herself recorded a couple of short personal video messages, which we duly uploaded. We then emailed our online supporter base to view these, with the hope that they would respond to her call to spread word of the campaign.

Whilst searching on YouTube to track down one of Joanna's videos I came across a Gurkha-related title that I didn't recognise. I clicked on it and it started to play. It was a short film made up of a series of slides – some were images of Gurkhas serving with the British Army over the ages, others were simple written phrases – with gently stirring Gurkha pipe music in the background. To say the video was moving is an understatement. It made the hairs stand up on the back of my neck. I played it again and again. The images were compelling, the music was stirring and the message was simple, but combined the overall effect was astonishingly powerful. I emailed Joanna and she too was incredibly moved. There was something indefinable about this film, short though it was, which captured the spirit of the campaign. But who had made it and why? Frustrated by my inability to navigate YouTube, I had to enlist the help of my step-daughter, Alice, to try and work out who had made this eloquent testament to our campaign.

Eventually, we tracked down one Darren Rafferty. I was never to meet Darren, though we spoke many times on the phone. It transpired that Darren lived in Northern Ireland and had a much loved but ailing uncle who had a massive affection for the Gurkhas. This, in turn, explained Darren's interest. He graciously allowed us to adopt his short film. Later in the campaign, Madan Gurung, with whom I was now close friends, offered up his cap badge to send to Darren's uncle as a token of our appreciation.

On one occasion, after one of our media events, I arranged for Joanna to speak with Darren, without any warning, just to say how grateful she and all of us were for his help and support and to explain just how much this film had meant to us. Joanna and I were sitting, as we so often did after a press conference or media event, on the small wall that surrounds the patch of grass known as College Green, directly opposite Parliament. It's the patch of earth used by the media to interview the 'talking heads' of MPs and Ministers. I dialled the number for Joanna and briefly explained to Darren that she wanted to talk to him. Darren has a very soft voice, so measured that you can't readily detect his mood or frame of mind, but even with this voice that gives so little away, you could just tell that for Darren this was his moment in the whirlwind of the campaign. It meant something to him.

Darren's film almost became our anthem. We linked it extensively to the Gurkha Justice campaign and with its help, by the time the final victory was secured, our humble website was to have harvested over 147,000 online signatures. It was simple, effective and powerful.

So on that High Court victory day, I resolved, behind Joanna on those famous steps and in such a position as to be seen and legible, we had to get a banner displaying the website name so that viewers would be able to read it in any live shots. Such are the logistical minutiae that campaign planning must deal with. I also knew that we needed a strong showing of as many senior and influential people as possible to add weight to the next push in the campaign.

Ever since those first few tentative days on the Gurkha campaign trail, the various leaders of the Lib Dem Party had offered considerable support to the cause. Charles Kennedy had given his blessing to a Gurkha delegation attending the Federal Conference in Bournemouth and had pushed the issue to Tony Blair at PMQs. Ming Campbell had offered support and advice and entertained the Gurkhas at Westminster. Latterly, Nick Clegg had done the same.

I called Nick Clegg's office to secure his attendance. They explained that he wouldn't be able to come as he had a prior engagement booked in Brussels. To be honest, I found this more than a little frustrating. Here was a major moment in a growing national campaign, something which he could, quite properly, share in – and he was going to miss it for a boring briefing in Brussels. I believed that more people would respect him for helping the Gurkhas than would appreciate his trip to Brussels.

But when the day came, I was thrilled to see Nick Clegg in attendance after all, along with Ming Campbell. There were about a thousand retired Gurkhas outside the court; a huge sea of media. I was soon fielding a whole series of calls from journalists booking interviews with Joanna. I took refuge in the coffee house directly across the road from the court while the sense of expectancy grew and grew, the crowds continued to swell and the media calls increased in frequency and urgency.

By now I was outside the court waiting for Joanna to arrive. Over the course of the campaign I had learnt that some sections of the media behave in a manner comparable to an RAF technique called the combat air patrol. This is where aircraft go out to the fringes of the theatre of operations and fly in a holding pattern, hoping to pounce on the enemy in a surprise move as they approach. To counter the journalistic version of these tactics, I had to spot Joanna before they did, get to her and act as a mixture of bodyguard, media assistant and – on occasion – handbag carrier and umbrella holder. Suddenly, Joanna emerged from a cab about 100 yards away. I managed to get to her just before the enemy raiders swooped and we made a slow progress to the court, doing an interview every few yards.

I stayed outside the court working away to try and make our victorious emergence work for the media – much organising had to be done. This time they had ladders with them to make sure they got their shots. The court officers were in and out, pressing for people and crews to be moved. Veterans from many different walks of service life came along, including Colonel Bob Stewart of Bosnia fame.

And then it was time.

There are few sounds that stir the soul like the Gurkha pipes. Imagine hearing them, at first quietly, then swirling and wafting eerily from the mighty entrance of the High Court. Suddenly, people were flooding out, pouring down the steps into the Strand. There was a seething mass of Gurkha blazers and hats. Gurkha wives and widows were ablaze in green saris and sparkling gold jewellery. All had tears in their eyes. These normally reserved men and women were hugging everyone in sight. The VC veterans Tul Badahur Pun and Lechiman Gurung were wheeled out and the press photographers and film crews formed a veritable amphitheatre in front of us as we prepared to acknowledge the moment.

I had sensed a degree of anxiety from the Howe & Co. team that Martin Howe should be the one to speak on the steps of the court following our victory. This I totally supported and we jointly made happen. For Martin and his team this was a defining moment in their legal careers. It would, in all probability, be the highest profile legal work they would ever undertake. More than that, they had engineered a true triumph for people to whom they were committed above and beyond the call of duty.

Martin spoke movingly. Then Joanna. I had briefed Joanna that she needed to celebrate the victory, but explained that this wasn't enough and that the campaign needed to go up a gear. She needed to launch the website in an explicit way, with a direct request for people to sign up, so that as many people as possible would be motivated to actually sign the petition and to spread the word to all their contacts. Getting a strong response to an internet petition is hugely dependent on a big initial sign up. By that means you have a ready source of people to email and ask to forward it on to their friends, thereby creating a snowball effect. As she spoke in that cauldron of celebration, with questions being fired from all angles, I was on tenterhooks. It would be so easy, even for a seasoned performer like Joanna, to make the required speeches but miss out the crucial exhortation to sign up to the website. I also knew that this had to work first time in front of BBC and Sky live news teams. I'd learnt that in pre-recorded pieces many broadcasters would edit out any references to campaign websites. Apparently, they don't see it as part of their remit to advertise such sites in an overt way. The advantage of live television is that it is immediately broadcast with no such opportunity for editing.

Joanna, as ever, pitched it perfectly. She acknowledged the remarkable legal victory but drove home the 'we need you to sign up' message. I was to later learn that within about thirty minutes of her speaking we had upwards of 10,000 online signatures. The power of celebrity, the media and of the internet was already beginning to fuse into a mighty campaigning force.

Eventually the crowds began to dissipate. The constant queue of TV crews wanting to interview Joanna had faded away and there was just a handful of the core campaigning team left milling about at the court entrance. Joanna had one last Radio 4 piece to do and that was from a tiny little studio in the body of the court buildings. As was to become the norm, I went with her to make sure that she found the right room and that all was going according to plan. This was a strange feeling. In my almost ten years of intense campaigning at parliamentary candidate level, it was usually I who had someone doing that for me.

With Joanna safely ensconced in the studio, I wandered back into the main body of the court building. Remarkably, it was totally deserted. I could see no one else about at all. I rested with my back against one of the walls and looked down the cavernous central aisle of the building with its great Gothic arches. I swear that it would have seemed quite normal if a medieval knight had wandered across the hall. The contrast between the silence that had now descended and the earlier, almost riotous celebrations was stark.

When I think back to these battles I often recall a much more recent conversation with a colleague during which we were looking at my approach to taking on a fight. I had told him that one of my favourite maxims was 'Never be intimated by the odds' – to which he replied, 'I didn't think you even stopped to work them out.' To be honest, I was quite pleased by his response.

Joanna emerged from a tiny side door, looking slightly disorientated by the lack of people. Seeing me at the end of the hallway, she walked down. Just for a few fleeting seconds we stared at each other, eye to eye, in that way that seems to happen only infrequently and exceptionally when you feel you might catch a glimpse of someone's inner soul. This was the point when I knew truly that Joanna would be in this to the end. She put her hand on my shoulder and we walked out together.

EIGHT

BLACK FRIDAY

N ews had reached us that the government was finally going to announce its new rules on Gurkha immigration. This was to be the result of the great High Court win in September of the previous year. In his ruling, the judge had specified that the government should come up with new guidelines within three months. However, the end of the year had gone by and a new one had started and still we heard nothing. As a result, the lawyers were forced to go back into action. On two occasions in early 2009 they went to court to try and force the government's hand. These were the only major parts of the campaign that I couldn't take part in or be present for. The pressures facing my transport company had risen and there were problems on so many fronts. We had to cut back on numbers of drivers and vehicles in an attempt to keep the business stable. I watched the media reports from the coal face at work.

Eventually, the lawyers succeeded: there would be a new policy. It would be revealed on Friday 24 April 2009. Joanna, Lynne, the legal team and I decided that we should be in or near Parliament to hear the new guidelines first hand. We were joined by the VCs Tul Bahadur Pun and Lechiman Gurung and a small number of other retired Gurkha veterans.

Our first hurdle was to try and find out how the policy would be announced. Would there be a ministerial announcement in the Commons? No. Would there be a written statement from a minister? No. Would it be formally lodged in the Commons Library? No. In a move that revealed so much about the government's view on this issue at this time, it chose instead to unveil the new guidelines on a page of the UK Border Agency website. Despite all the campaigning work and parliamentary lobbying that we had done, despite all the media interest and support across the country, the government had decided to do it in this unseemly way – there was no sense of occasion. Was this an attempt to get the new policy out in the open without anyone noticing? Or was it a subtle way of making it clear what little import they attached to the issue? Either way, it looked a pretty poor show to us.

The next problem was trying to get some web access so that we could print out and read the new policy. There were we, stood outside Parliament – we had no means of logging onto the internet to see this new web page. One of the staff members of Nick Clegg's office kindly volunteered to get it for us.

When the printed sheets arrived, we almost clambered over each in our rush to see what the government's response would be. It was shocking. What we read felt like a missile striking at the heart of the campaign. This was to be our Black Friday. The new policy contained five main points that, if satisfied by a pre-1997 Gurkha, would serve as grounds to allow settlement:

- The Gurkha must be able to demonstrate a period of three years of their service for which they were based in the UK;
- That they had 'close family ties' to others who were already in the UK;
- That the Gurkha had received a level one to three decoration for bravery;
- That they had a total service period of at least twenty years;
- That they had a medical condition of a chronic nature that could be proven to have resulted from their service.

The more we pored over this document, the more terrible it became. We were dumbfounded. These criteria were almost impossible for any retired Gurkha to meet. This had all the hallmarks of a cynical attempt to do the absolute minimum required to get around the High Court judgment. Part of that judgment had said that the rules relating to pre-1997 retirees were unclear; the government had made them clearer, but it had certainly not made them fairer. Martin and David confirmed our worst fears. This would help practically no Gurkha who had retired before 1997.

By now, the interested media were gathering outside. We collected our thoughts and walked towards the double doors at the St Stephen's entrance still framing our various responses. We had to carry the wheelchairs holding the VCs down the stone steps and then we were out, the media stiffening up as they waited to hear what we had to say, microphones thrust forward. Joanna was both furious and upset and as she delivered our response she was fighting back tears. On a couple of occasions they broke through.

Joanna used the word ashamed to sum up her feelings about this document. One by one, she exposed how each of the five key points that made up the new policy offered little hope for the pre-1997 retired Gurkha community. The overwhelming majority of retired Gurkhas were not allowed to serve in Britain for three years. If they had come at all, it would normally have been for two. Joanna moved on. If most Gurkhas were not allowed to live here, how could those wishing to come to Britain have formed any 'close' family ties? The third criterion, that relating to bravery decorations, was one of the most offensive of the five. This was probably an attempt to ensure that the government could avoid any 'difficult' campaigns for highly decorated Gurkha veterans, such as the one it had faced in the case of Tul Bahadur Pun VC.

The message it sent out was that only Gurkhas who had been decorated for their bravery were worthy of being allowed in. How would this feel to the thousands of Gurkha veterans who just never had the chance to show the kind of bravery that merited a medal? Why should they be excluded from these new provisions? One by one Joanna worked through the criteria. The fourth would have been funny if it were not part of an ultimately devastating outcome. Retired Gurkhas who had served twenty years could qualify to settle in Britain – only those that make officer grade are even allowed to serve for twenty years. The rank and file serve for fifteen. The final point was equally ridiculous: retired Gurkhas who could show that they were suffering from a chronic illness relating to their service could qualify – how on earth could such a link be proved?

I listened to Joanna set out why all of this was totally unacceptable and tried to imagine what collection of people had managed to come up with this new policy. I guessed that few had ever served in the military or held any appreciation of what is supposed to be a military covenant.

David Enright of Howe & Co. then gave one of his virtuoso performances. David is a great speech-giver, with his powerful Northern Irish accent. He has that rare ability to catch the mood of the moment with a few powerful words and phrases. Slowly and deliberately, as only a true orator can, he built up the level of anger in his voice until his words rang out across the face of Parliament: 'The Immigration Minister [Phil Woolas] should hang his head so low that it could touch his boots.' We had thought the status of the High Court ruling would mean that the government response would at least be delivered by a minister. However, no elected politician of any level was charged with handling the issue. In my few words, I asked where the minister responsible for these new guidelines was on such a day as this. Unbeknownst to me, as the BBC News Channel cameras panned away from me, the programme's coverage went straight to Phil Woolas, the Immigration Minister, who was away on business 'up North'.

This was undeniably a setback. We were pressed on what we would do next. Thinking on my feet, I told the media that we would now be increasing the amount of lobbying we were doing. All our previous calls for help and support had been to show the government the very high level of support for the campaign across the country. Now, I resolved, we needed to turn up the heat on MPs and ministers to new and unprecedented levels. Once the media had left, we all took stock. It was easy to say that we would not give up, far harder to work out what to do and how to do it.

LECHIMAN GURUNG VC

Drift back in time with me, if you will. We are in the dying days of the Second World War out in the Far East. We are overlooking a trench at the forward edge of the British position at Taungdaw, Burma. Lechiman Gurung is in that trench along with two comrades. They are facing an overwhelming force of Japanese infantry numbering many hundreds.

A hand grenade is thrown by the Japanese towards the British position. In an act of incredible bravery, Lechiman catches it and throws it back. Within a short time, a second grenade is thrown and Lechiman catches this too and throws it back. In the murderous heat of battle, a third grenade is thrown by the Japanese. But Lechiman is unable to return this one to its owner. It explodes in his right hand. His wounds are horrendous. His hand is shattered and his face, body and legs are severely damaged. His two comrades are seriously wounded.

Lechiman fought on for four long hours, literally single-handed. With supreme courage, he repelled wave after wave of Japanese soldiers. When he ran out of ammunition, he stuck his Kukri knife in the lip of the trench and shouted, 'Come and fight me, I'm a Gurkha.' At the end of the action, it was reported that there were over thirty Japanese dead in front of his position. For this, Lechiman was awarded the highest military honour for courage in the face of the enemy, the Victoria Cross.

I first met Lechiman at one of our demonstrations in Westminster. Gurkhas are not renowned for their height, but I remember being struck by just how tiny Lechiman Gurung looked sat in his wheelchair. I later heard that as a young man he was so short that he may even have been beneath the height required to enter service. Lechiman and I only ever spoke briefly. However, like his colleague, Tul Bahadur Pun VC, he was always present in the campaign. They both attended rally after rally, march after march. Good weather, bad weather – they were always there. Two members of the London Taxi Benevolent Association for War Disabled, Gary Belsey and Dave Snow, had heard about the Gurkha campaign on local radio and phoned up Howe & Co. to give their support. They offered to ferry these heroes around to our various demonstrations and events free of charge in their black cabs. Their unfailing support and commitment were inspiring.

I occasionally get invited to talk to audiences about the Gurkha Justice campaign. Sometimes it is groups like the Women's Institute, whose members have a strong interest in the Gurkhas; other times its businesses and organisations who want to know how the campaign came into being and what made it so effective. I very often start off my talk by simply telling the story of Lechiman. No introduction – just what happened. I can tell it within seconds. The audience sinks into that silent concentration that is born of a sense of awe. They are looking at a picture beamed up behind me of a frail elderly man sat awkwardly in a wheelchair. They can see the bar of medals across his chest. Sometimes I have seen tears gently start to roll down people's faces as the story unfolds.

And then I tell them that despite his valour – a valour of the most extraordinary kind, a valour that after all the intervening years still amazes – Lechiman was not welcomed in Britain. That he received the response all retired Gurkhas get: he 'did not have a close enough tie to the UK to qualify for a visa'. Yes, really. At this stage the tears roll down people's faces even more. To be honest, though I have relayed Lechiman's story many a time, it still makes me shiver when I think that our country has treated these people so badly. How on earth could we have displayed that level of sheer ingratitude and heartlessness? I struggle to imagine how the people who made these rules, who wrote these letters of rejection, could ever have allowed it to go unchallenged.

....

NINE

PARLIAMENT TO THE RESCUE

———◆———

I n the aftermath of Black Friday, our mood was low. We were sitting on the grass of College Green. Joanna was having a cigarette. We often ended up here after our demonstrations and events. If sustenance was required, we could walk just a few yards to the coffee bar in the Jewel Tower, the ruin just opposite Parliament that attracts a steady stream of curious tourists.

Then my mobile rang. This was what is now my old mobile phone, long since replaced in active service by the dreaded (but very useful) BlackBerry. Inanimate object though that old Nokia is, I've never got rid of it. In its busy life, it received calls from David Cameron, Nick Clegg, Gordon Brown and Joanna Lumley. I used to wonder just how much impact a few committed people with a couple of mobile phones could have. Now I know – so I keep it as a memento of that fact.

It was Nick Clegg's office on the line. The Liberal Democrats had an Opposition Day motion opening scheduled for 29 April and Nick's team were thinking that using it to open debate on the Gurkhas would add political weight to the campaign. Such motions are considered valuable as they gave the opposition parties an opportunity to air an issue and apply pressure to the government. They're not generally expected actually to be carried on the floor of the House – but then again, there was always a chance, however small. From the party perspective, the issue was already high profile and it was likely that the debate would attract even more media interest. It would show that the Lib Dems were leading the pack on this issue.

I conferred with Kieran and the other lawyers. A smoking Joanna agreed that the motion would be a natural extension of our political campaign.

As ever in the run-up to significant events in the campaign, emails flew between us late into the night. Nick's office needed help framing the motion so that it accurately reflected the aims of the campaign.

On the Sunday before the debate, Lynne and I had friends over for a barbecue at our Folkestone home. It was a classic scene of relaxed summer fun; but that afternoon ended up being far from typical. I was aware that the only realistic chance we would have to win the debate in Parliament would be to get the Conservatives on side. So that afternoon I broke away from the merriment to speak with Nick Clegg by phone.

Nick and I did not know each other well, though we had worked closely on the Gurkha campaign and so had a good rapport. Nick had entered politics by a very different route to mine. I had always wanted to be an MP who had come up through what I regarded as normal life; not the path of public school, university, political research job, MEP through to 'safe' seat, following on from a previous MP. Though I had been to university, that was against a backdrop of 'working class lad made good'.

So here on that Sunday afternoon, at home cooking burgers, I found myself in the surreal position of talking to Nick Clegg, the leader of the third largest political party in the UK, trying to choreograph the events and media that would undoubtedly surround a Commons vote.

There was no concept of Nick being high and mighty. It was to his very great credit that he had taken a lead on this issue right from the time of my first approach to him and, like me, he was focused on the matter at hand. I explained that for this event to have impact, we needed the Conservatives involved too. Did he feel comfortable with this? We would need to work together to prevent any unpleasant last-minute upstaging by Cameron and his team. I reassured Nick that I would plan the media approach carefully. At that time, the national press could often be dismissive of the Lib Dems and their leader. It was entirely possible that, in the event of a win, the media would focus on the role played by David Cameron and relegate Nick and his role to the sidelines. A long line of Lib Dem leaders had given this issue their support. It would be politically outrageous if the Tories were portrayed as the Gurkhas' knights in shining armour, when, in reality, they were very much the johnnies-come-lately.

I switched calls and spoke with Joanna. I explained to her that whilst we could clearly see that the campaign had to be non-party political, there were certain problems that our joint Lib Dem/Conservative strategy could have for Nick. She understood.

By now the burgers were getting a little overcooked. *The Sun* rang, asking if there was any real chance of the Commons vote being won. How on earth could I know? When in doubt, be certain. 'Yes,' I said, 'a real chance. We are determined that the retired Gurkhas will see the Lib Dems and Conservatives lining up together.' Then it was time for a quick flip of the burgers and sausages before another call with Nick – by which time our guests were more than a little bemused by the sheer volume of calls.

Joanna herself offered to make contact with David Cameron's office. This was perhaps for the best – I already felt slightly torn suggesting, indeed encouraging, my leader, Nick Clegg, to work so openly with the Conservatives. The Tories and the Lib Dems were not close bed fellows – how things would change after the 2010 general election! – but if we could get all of them together there was a chance, a slight chance, that enough Labour MPs would either abstain or even vote against the government for us to achieve a result. Even if we lost the vote, the political imagery of the Lib Dems and Conservatives standing shoulder to shoulder on the issue would be a strong signal to our Gurkha veterans that a future government would be able to deliver justice.

In my mind, that future government would probably be Conservative, and the Machiavellian part of me thought that this vote would be an opportunity to tie the Conservatives to the cause. We had had some very supportive signs from the Tories, but also some worrying indications, particularly since some of their MPs seemed to see Gurkha rights as more of an immigration matter than an issue with a clear overriding moral imperative. I certainly felt that Damian Green, the shadow Immigration Minister, was a long way from seeing this as a contravention of the British military covenant, rather than of the British borders. But if we could only persuade the Conservatives as a whole to make a public pledge of support for the campaign, it would be very hard for them to back track should they indeed form the next administration.

In my mind's eye I had framed the image that we needed to see after the Commons vote, win or lose: Joanna flanked by David Cameron and Nick Clegg. It was easy to imagine such a picture, but how on earth was I to make it happen? Even if both sides were agreeable, the basic logistics of actually getting the two leaders together in one place after the vote would be a challenge. On top of that, I was worried about whether the media would even pick up on the significance of the image. In fact, if we lost the vote, I was worried that they would give it a miss altogether.

I did as much as I could to make sure that the initiative would not be hijacked by the Conservatives. I reminded myself that when Michael Howard was well placed to take on the issue as MP for Folkestone & Hythe, he did not. Further, when he became leader of the Conservative Party and could have championed the cause at the despatch box, he did not. It would have bordered on political criminality if, at this late stage of the campaign, the Conservatives were able to jump on the bandwagon and make political capital out of it. So much of national politics is tribal and I felt an obligation to protect my party. That said, this issue was so strong that nothing, certainly not party political tribalism, could or should stand in its way.

TEN

PLOTTING

———◆———

We sat in the music room of Joanna's London home, the air heavy with cigarette smoke. Around the table were gathered Joanna, Kieran, Darren Briddock, Tim Prater and his business partner, Matt Raines, and me. The item under discussion was how to handle the aftermath of our next major event, the Commons vote.

We had won in the courts, we had won in the media, we had won in the hearts and minds of the British people. Yet it seemed that the government would continue to try and hold out and refuse the right of settlement to those Gurkhas who had retired pre-1997. Tomorrow would be the vote in Parliament. To win the vote would be fabulous, but unlikely. The odds were slight. The government whips would almost certainly live up to their name and the motion would fall. However, there would be positives. There would certainly be strong media coverage and we would also be able to see which MPs spoke and voted in our favour. Therefore, we had to plan on how best to handle losing.

And so to details. Darren told the group that we had a sound system available to us during the day. I confirmed that we had the necessary permits to use it. You might think that operating a sound system in the open air, albeit near to the Palace of Westminster, would pose few problems. You'd be wrong. The use of loud hailers and powered PA systems is regulated by the events team at Westminster City Council. You have to apply in writing and pay a fee, and you also have to give twenty-eight days' notice. Very often in our campaign events were planned with less than twenty-eight minutes' notice, never mind twenty-eight days. Over the years, I lost count of the number of times we had to fight the switchboard and internal phone system of Westminster City Council to get through to the relevant officers. At times, I thought that Westminster Council was being deliberately difficult – they were more of a deterrent to demonstrations than a water cannon.

After the logistics and technology of the sound system came the choreography of the day. Whatever happened in the vote after the Opposition Day motion, our dream image would be Cameron, Clegg and Joanna surrounded by a sea of Gurkhas. We explained to Joanna that we might need to stay inside the Palace of Westminster for a time in order to 'form up' before we went outside. If Cameron came out first he could (inadvertently I'm sure) end up seizing the media momentum. If Clegg came out without Joanna we might not capitalise on the media interest. There was still considerable uncertainty as to whether Mr Cameron would be able to take part in the photo shoot at all, as he had a prior engagement scheduled with the Hungarian Prime Minister. Generally, it was Kieran and I who worked together to organise this sort of event. However, on this occasion we knew it would all happen very quickly and Joanna would be the only person who would be able to make it work. I remember that at this point she flicked her hair back and came out with one of the great quotes of the campaign: 'Can I do that? I'm only an actress.'

Our attention now turned to what we would do next after the inevitability of losing the Commons vote. Our band of plotters were trying to find the lever, the threat, the thing that would force the reluctant government to buckle. The whole emphasis of the campaign had, up until now, been all about persuasion and charm. Now the mood seemed to have changed. There were the first signs of a hardening of our position.

Tim had come up with an idea, which he had suggested to me a few days earlier – the Nuclear Option. It was quite brilliant. Audacious? Yes. Risky? Certainly. I loved it.

Momentum in successful campaigns can only ever get more powerful. If you start to lose energy it becomes increasingly difficult to continue going forward. The problem with campaigns that gain momentum quickly, like ours, is that the next event, challenge or initiative has to be even more dramatic than the last to maintain a feeling of ever-advancing progress. We had marched everywhere there was to march. We had petitioned Number 10 to the point they thought we were the postman.

Now we asked Joanna if she would consider, if all else failed, standing at the next general election against Gordon Brown in his own seat. The seasoned Lib Dem campaigners around the table, me included, would form the core of the election campaign team. Darren would be her agent. I would be campaign manager. Tim would provide IT support and back-up, as well as considerable campaigning and design skills. Joanna would be an independent candidate campaigning on the strength of a single issue – Gurkha Justice.

The Liberal Democrats and the Liberals before them had never managed to make a significant break-through at national level in the history of modern politics. It had often been threatened. Many remember the battle cry of David Steel in 1981 when he was leader of the Liberal Party: 'Go back to your constituencies and prepare for government.' But it had never actually been delivered. That lack of a national break-through belied the fact that the Lib Dems had, over the years, produced some great parliamentary campaigns. Plenty of seats had been snatched from both of the larger parties over the years. Chris Rennard (now a

Lord), in particular, had masterminded a whole series of spectacular by-election wins, often against incredible odds. A generation of Lib Dems had learned their campaigning skills from Chris; some were now sat around this table.

However, there was a potential downside to this plan for all of us as Lib Dems: we would have to give up membership of our party. Under the rules of the Lib Dems (and, I think, of the other parties) you cannot remain a member if you actively support and campaign for another person or party standing against the official Lib Dem candidate in an election.

The lawyers seemed a bit baffled by the dilemma that we Lib Dem plotters were facing. After many years of working and standing for a party, you develop close ties and friendships. You become part of the tribe – whether that is to a greater or lesser extent depends on your personality. In my experience, the party with the strongest group identity in politics is the Conservatives. When threatened – for example, by a strong challenger from another party – the Tories display all the characteristics of the inhabitants of a termite mound when poked with a stick: they get very angry, very quickly, and always stick together. Anyone who leaves the party, who embarrasses it or challenges it overtly is ex-communicated like a mediaeval heretic. By comparison, the least tribal party is the Liberal Democrats. Indeed, often the Lib Dems are so 'un-tribal' that getting them to go in the same direction feels near impossible. My own personal feeling is that, in terms of effective politics, the less emphasis placed on toeing the party line, the more flexibility and freedom there is to genuinely solve problems. Nonetheless, we knew that making this decision would almost certainly mean being excluded from our tribe, and that was not something to be taken lightly.

But the angst and difficulty that this might cause us was irrelevant if the lady herself wouldn't agree to stand. We outlined the proposal's potential to a somewhat startled Joanna. I don't think she had ever imagined this as a possibility, but she didn't dismiss it out of hand. You could almost see her mind working overtime on what this would mean. It was a viable plan. We had the skills and knowledge to put together a powerful election campaign. In addition, we reckoned that there would be several thousand retired Gurkhas willing to canvass and deliver election leaflets for Joanna until their feet bled.

Joanna expressed concern about what would happen if she actually won. Despite the fact that we were often fighting against politicians, Joanna had never criticised them in any negative way. Though the emerging expenses scandal had pushed the reputation of many MPs to a new low in the eyes of the public, Joanna always acknowledged the important job they did. She did not want to trivialise the role of MP for Gordon Brown's constituency of Kirkcaldy & Cowdenbeath. The people there deserved a dedicated MP who could and would work for them with absolute dedication. Joanna would not be able to do that.

As ever, team Howe & Co. were full of ideas. Sometimes when the lawyers were present they could, unintentionally, be quite dominating and it was difficult to maintain our focus on the key messages. Many a time, after such meetings, I had to set out my thoughts more clearly for Joanna separately by phone or by email. Tonight was such a night. The concept that we were exploring needed to be fully explained, so that Joanna had enough information to form a considered view – and we all needed time to understand what it would mean for each of us and for the campaign.

I felt that Joanna was convinced but troubled. This was all very easy and exciting to talk about, but it would be a mammoth commitment to deliver a comprehensive campaign against a sitting Prime Minister – even though we might have half the population of Nepal on our side.

With the main business of the meeting over we were able to relax for a short while. Whenever the team was together in large numbers there was always a lot of laughter. The camaraderie between us was huge. We talked late into the night, amply sustained by refreshments supplied by Joanna, and afterwards Tim and Matt were able to give me and Darren a lift back to Folkestone. As we drove out of south-east London and down the M20, we knew that the battle was about to move on.

ELEVEN

THE COMMONS VOTE

———◆———

The day of the vote arrived and in the morning Joanna met with David Cameron and his shadow Immigration Minister, Damian Green. Joanna and I conferred afterwards. How had it gone? Again, the line kept coming through that maybe the Conservative's new points-based immigration system might deal with this issue. Joanna, quite rightly, was discreet about what was actually said in the meeting. I suspect that she was able to impart a degree of resolve to the Conservative leadership. I believe the message was that without a very strong whip and the resulting strong showing of Tory MPs in the Chamber, the vote would most definitely be lost.

We gathered on that Wednesday in Old Palace Yard. I estimate about 1,000 retired Gurkhas had assembled.

I spent a great deal of time managing expectations. I was concerned that the Gurkhas would be devastated if we were to lose this vote, when it would be better viewed as just another step along a long road. So many people who have grown up with our political system hold the understandable but mistaken view that a victory on the floor of the House of Commons translates automatically into a change in the law. I sensed that some of the Gurkhas might be of that frame of mind. I explained that even if we won the vote, it would not be binding on the government. Understandably, the Gurkhas were baffled by this. To be honest, so was I. It seemed perfectly reasonable that if the democratically elected House voted on a matter, the government should be bound to honour their decision.

A gentleman approached me with a genuine Kukri knife and asked if he could give it to Joanna. The knife had been handed to him by a dying Gurkha soldier. He had kept it ever since. Joanna took the knife from its sheath and held it aloft. Surrounded by a sea of Gurkha veterans, she looked like a cross between the Statue of Liberty and Boudicca. This image was to become one of the great press shots of the entire campaign. Unbelievably, on a subsequent campaign event, the police told me that a member of the public had actually phoned Scotland Yard to complain that Joanna Lumley had been seen live on television with an offensive weapon.

Odd snippets of the debate were being fed back to those of us out in Old Palace Yard by our supporters who were in the café and lobby area watching it on the internal TV system. The first encouraging sign was that the House was packed – Joanna's morning visit to see Mr Cameron appeared to have worked. So often in the past, when we had brought in Private Members' Bills, we had been disappointed with the turnout of MPs. This time it was different.

Throughout the debate, we learnt that the government was lobbying hard to try and stop Labour MPs abstaining or voting against the government. Rumours spread, eventually substantiated, that the Home Office was circulating a document trying to offer limited concessions – what might be considered a 'buy-off'. Government whips, meanwhile, were allegedly intercepting Labour members en route to the chamber, reminding them of the need to support their PM and government. The folklore of Westminster is full of stories about the lengths that party whips will go to dissuade rebellion. There is often a mixture of threat – 'It won't be good for your career' – and, conversely, enticement – 'There may be a position for you...' There is a real conflict between a sense of self-preservation and loyalty to the party and a desire to vote in line with one's conscience. This is the side of our political system that seems completely out of step with the concept of Parliament as a crucible of free-thinking debate.

One Labour MP who was doing his best to follow his conscience was Martin Salter MP, the chair of the All-Party Working Group on Gurkha Affairs. He tried hard to persuade the assembled press pack and the retired Gurkhas that losing the vote wouldn't be the end of the world. We had, he explained, kept the cause on the political agenda. I think most people would acknowledge that Martin had done excellent work on behalf of the campaign, particularly in ensuring that the influential Home Affairs Committee (HAC) under Keith Vaz MP took the issue seriously.

The hearings before the HAC had been a key element in our overall campaign. It was a forum that allowed us to probe and question the government's position and Mr Vaz was to become quite a star in his role as chair. There were two key meetings of the HAC that examined the Gurkha issue. At one of these meetings, part way through, Joanna was fascinated to see Mr Vaz produce an apple from his case, peel and consume it with great aplomb without so much as a pause in proceedings.

At another, this one packed with public and media, having previously heard Joanna describe how she had attempted many times to secure a Prime Ministerial meeting by letter, at least two handwritten and personally delivered, Mr Vaz now questioned her publicly: 'Do you want to meet the Prime Minister?' Joanna answered with a 'Yes' that was simultaneously breathy, pleading, dignified and almost haunting – positively Shakespearian.

At the same meeting, Joanna casually mentioned that the immense support expressed from all across society included a member of the Royal Family. Perfect timing. From the point of view of keeping the media interested, this was sublime. Just as the campaign needed a little extra petrol thrown on the fire, she provided it. Before the word 'Family' had left her lips the press benches were suddenly all leaning forward with pricked ears, scribbling their copy frenziedly. Reports speculating on who the Royal might be were all across the newspapers the next day.

It was these meetings, too, that we saw one of the main operators for the other side in action. Kevan Jones MP, a junior Defence Minister with wide rang-ing responsibilities for Gurkha matters, gave his evidence to the committee barely managing to hide what appeared to be utter contempt for the campaign and all who fought with it. I watched from the back of the room as he said his piece. His most disparaging remark, which to me was a window on his inner think-ing, was said with a sneer: 'You can now buy a Hoodie with Gurkha Justice on it.' It was clear that Mr Jones was a bit of a 'bother boy' in a smart suit.

But despite all Martin's hard work in making these meetings possible, many were left surprised and angered by his contribution on the day of the Commons vote; not his finest Gurkha hour. Not only was Martin a Labour MP, he was widely regarded as a senior Labour Party figure. He was in an excruciating position, but many of us felt that he slipped back at this point to being an apologist for the government. Though Martin insisted that even in the event of loss the government was listening, the assembled Gurkhas struggled to understand why he had only abstained and not voted against his party.

The crowd became subdued. Then David Enright took the platform. If David hadn't become a solicitor, I am certain he would have been a film star in the mould of Kenneth Branagh. David would have done an equally good Henry V – if only his Irish heritage would let him. He told the assembled Gurkhas that we would 'never, never, never' (in the model of Ian Paisley) let them down.

The Opposition Day debate was over. The MPs had voted and the result was about to be declared. We gathered in tense silence in the very small, wood-lined office of the Lib Dem whip, Paul Burstow MP. Joanna had been listening to the debate from the gallery but had come to join us to hear the result. She and I exchanged ideas on how best to go forward from here. Would we have to put our Nuclear Option into action? If so, should we announce it today or in a few days' time? How would we handle the intense disappointment that the Gurkhas would surely feel? Joanna told me that Iain Duncan Smith had passed her as she made her way out to us and had offered strong congratulations but felt he had to prepare her for the disappointment of losing the actual vote. After all, it was over thirty years since a government had suffered such a defeat.

As the tellers walked down the central aisle of the House of Commons, someone must have seen the result on the paper in the teller's hands, because the Opposition side started to wave their Order Papers – the customary sign of celebration and victory. A voice from somewhere in the room, and I still don't know whose voice it was, exclaimed, 'We've won!' Everyone suddenly tensed like a parade of soldiers that has been at ease but is now ordered to attention. But we needed confirmation. In my mind it took an age, an absolute age, for the tellers to arrive before the Speaker and for the ritual reading out of the result.

I have only ever been in one car crash in my life. Many years ago I was the front seat passenger in the Mini that belonged to my wonderful middle sister Pauline. We were driving down Nangreave Road in our home town of Stockport when the brakes failed as we approached the back end of a car stopped at the traffic lights. My abiding memory of the resulting crash is of everything going suddenly into slow motion. It was just like watching a replay on *Match of the Day*. Apparently, this happens because your brain works out that what's happening is pretty amazing and you start to think in a way that makes everything slow down. Crammed into the Lib Dem whip's office that day, I was to feel this crazy slow motion effect all over again.

The tellers duly halted in front of the Deputy Speaker. The 'aye's to the right, 267; the 'no's to the left, 246. When it came, it felt like everyone in the room had jumped up in the air and been captured in rapture by a flash freeze-frame. Joanna was at least six inches above the floor. The lawyers were in every contortion a football team might be when they have scored the winner in a Cup Final.

Damian Green for the Conservatives and David Heath for the Lib Dems were up within seconds pressing home the point that this was a 'historic' defeat and demanding urgent statements from government ministers about how they were going to react to the result and the 'clear will of the House'. Even the Deputy Speaker was moved to acknowledge the importance of this vote.

There was wide-eyed, jaw-dropped, awesome joy. I'm not renowned for being a 'huggy' person but today was different. I hugged Holly, Polly, Leena and Zeena, all Lib Dem staff members – a great rhyme for a team. David Heath MP, the Lib Dem Member for Frome, burst into the office with a smile so wide it could have stretched from Westminster to his constituency. In slightly less than the full formal parliamentary parlance, he shouted out, 'I've waited twelve years to do that to these bastards.' (That's beat the government in a Commons vote.) Lib Dem MP after Lib Dem MP poured into the office. Hugs and delirium everywhere.

There had been many powerful moments in the campaign to date. There would be many more. However, the victory that day on the floor of the House of Commons was one of the most profound.

That we had managed to pull off a defeat of the government on the floor of the House was stunning. To have done it with our small resources made the moment even more striking. The whole Westminster lobbying industry exists to try to get information through to MPs and build up enough support to effect or change legislation. Millions of pounds are spent every year by all sorts of different organisations in order to raise their profile or to influence some small but, to those affected, important piece of legislation. For most, this can take years of effort; in this mad dash of a campaign we had generated such interest and momentum that the two opposition parties had been persuaded to come together in support of our issue and over fifty Labour MPs had been moved to rebel against their own government.

The action of those fifty Labour MPs needs special mention. A rebellion in the voting lobby is not under-taken lightly, since it usually incurs the wrath of the leadership and of the whips. I am sure that some of the rebelling Labour MPs voted as they did because of their principled stand on the issue; others will have done so as a result of the phenomenal amount of correspondence they received from the tens of thou-sands of supporters across the country. In my book, both reasons are equally valid.

In a political sense, it was as if the earth had moved. Our campaign had grown from its first faltering steps, through legal battles, petitions and marches, under the growing glare of the media spotlight, to this moment. We had crossed a line. Amongst all the pres-sure of normal parliamentary business and the chaos of political life, our issue had won through. You could almost feel the impact on the government.

Parliament is often mocked. Heavens knows how poorly some of its members have served. All that said, it is the centre of our democracy. I recall reading that Margaret Thatcher felt, on some occasions, that the House had an almost mystical feeling when it confronted the great issues of the day. In her case, I believe that she was referring to the debate at the start of the Falklands War. Today, the House had found its voice and spoken. It had taken a stand against the government. It had acted for its people.

We had planned that whatever the outcome, win or lose, Joanna would leave Parliament with Nick Clegg and David Cameron and that the three of them would address the assembled media and our Gurkha friends waiting in Old Palace Yard. We had thought for much of the day that we would most likely be explaining that the vote, though lost, had been an important step in the campaign and that the fact that Nick Clegg and David Cameron were united on the issue meant that we would be victorious in a future Parliament. Instead, it was in a swirl of victory that we streamed out of the office and Joanna, as choreographed, led Nick Clegg and David Cameron out through the St Stephen's entrance to face the wall of media.

The mass of Gurkhas were on the other side of the road. Though some distance away, we could hear their roar as we emerged from Parliament. I had wanted to get Joanna, David and Nick out of the building and across the road before they spoke with the media – that way the impromptu press conference would take place in the midst of an army of retired Gurkhas. I had no chance. BBC and Sky were directly outside the door; that slowed our progress almost to a dead stop. Now I had a dilemma. Did we stick with the original plan and cross the road, or take the media there and then? In the end, the sheer media crush made the decision for me. We halted. The whole scene was live on air. Joanna paid tribute to the MPs then graciously, and most importantly, handed over to Nick Clegg before David Cameron. To his great credit, Cameron spoke well and made sure to acknowledge Nick's role.

Joanna, Nick and David paid eloquent testimony to the significance of the result. A few journalists raised the point that, in a technical sense, the vote was not binding on the government. Whilst true, we all believed that no government could defy the will of the House when it had been so dramatically expressed.

Then the group strode off to cross the road outside Parliament and address the great throng of Gurkhas.

Joanna stood on the base of the statue in the middle of Old Palace Yard, flanked by Clegg and Cameron. Here, the order of speeches was most diplomatically handled by my colleague Darren Briddock, a great help in so many of our events. He simply passed the microphone to Nick Clegg first, thrusting it into his hand saying, 'Nick, it's live...'

TWELVE

JOANNA MEETS MR BROWN
6/5/2009

———•———

always knew that at some point Joanna would have to meet Gordon Brown. In the end, the only person who would be able to force this through would be the Prime Minister himself. How to make this happen?

Joanna had written several letters to the Prime Minister. One she had delivered herself, written in her own handwriting. Another had been passed to the PM's Red Box by a supportive MP. A further letter had been written by Joanna and me together and then posted. None of the three solicited a reply.

Then I had an idea. I was accompanying a work colleague so that he could drop his car off to be serviced and the idea came into my head whilst waiting for him. Why don't we just phone Gordon Brown and ask for a meeting? Simple! The more I thought about it, the more I could see that this offered up a real possibility of provoking a reaction. The Gurkha issue was running in all the media on the wave of our success at the Commons vote. On the previous day, Joanna had expressed regret that her letters to the PM were unanswered. I had the phone number for the Number 10 switchboard. When should we do this? How about straight away?

I called Joanna and put the plan to her. Her response? 'But darling, I'm cleaning the oven in my marigolds.' Gamely she set them aside and made the call. Four hours later, Joanna Lumley was face-to-face with Gordon Brown. It had worked. Heaven knows what the switchboard operator made of the call!

Downing Street had seemed reluctant for her to meet the PM at Number 10. Instead, the meeting was convened for his Westminster office. My plans for the day abandoned, I hurtled up to London to see Joanna before she went in.

Joanna was the only person from our side in the meeting. The Prime Minister made it clear that he was minded to hold firm on the 1997 date. He repeated the government's grounds for doing this. One reason given was the alleged huge cost of £4.5 billion for goodness knows what. We suspected that the MoD was behind this figure as they were to play on it during many other meetings. Despite this, the Prime Minister said enough for Joanna to work with – in the face of her pleas he assured her that he would look at the issue further.

After the meeting, Joanna was unusually lost in thought.

News of the get-together had percolated out to the media. I received a flurry of calls: 'What was happening?', 'Is the PM offering a deal?' ran the questions. When Joanna went out to brief the press she cleverly played on the tiny fragments of half-positive things that had been said. She praised the Prime Minister. She told the assembled press gathering that he was a good man with great integrity and that he was personally taking the matter into his own hands. She boxed him into a corner with a degree of precision that a fine carpenter would have been proud of. She left anyone interested in this story with the impression that Joanna Lumley knew that the PM would not let her down. Such was the power and strength of her identification with the issue, and the identification of our supporters with her, that she rather brilliantly made it clear that if the PM didn't solve the issue he would be letting the country down.

Within minutes, Paul Lambert of the BBC was talking to me. The press office at Number 10, he said, had a different interpretation of what had been said at the meeting. I knew that what they thought mattered very little. What was important was how the public would react. The whole country was now looking to the PM, waiting to see what his next move would be. I imagine the spin doctors of Number 10 were trying to work out the scale of damage that would result from Joanna ever having to go back onto to College Green to say that she was disappointed.

GYANENDRA RAI

Gyanendra Rai went to the Falklands in 1982. He was part of the task force despatched by Margaret Thatcher to retake the islands from their Argentinean invaders. Gyanendra was seriously injured at Bluff Cove when a large piece of shrapnel pierced his back. He was in serious danger. Only by the actions of the remarkable naval surgeon Dr Rick Jolly OBE did he survive.

Gyanendra Rai had to leave the British Army as a result of his wounds. He received no medical benefits and he did not receive a pension. He returned to Nepal. He was in constant pain and living in poverty. So poor and so difficult were the conditions that he and his family had to endure that he was to lose his first wife after childbirth. He had to carry her for six hours to try and find medical treatment. She died on the way. Despite the testimonial from Commander Jolly that Corporal Rai needed expert medical supervision, his multiple applications to enter Britain were refused. I was to finally meet him out in Kathmandu, when he pushed himself to the front of a large crowd just to say 'thank you'. Totally humbling. He now lives in Britain but has still had to pay thousands and thousands of pounds for his visas.

Tul Bahadur Pun VC, now deceased, who is believed to have played a role in saving the life of Major James Lumley. I always felt humbled in his presence.

I lost count of the number of times we marched up Whitehall. This was one of our largest marches. Darren Briddock (far left) was 'marshall in chief', responsible for making sure we adhered to the rules and were not placed in handcuffs by PC MacInally.

A defining moment in modern political television. That is quite a glare...

MPs and Lords braved the traffic and came out to Parliament Square to sign a pledge banner. Baroness Trumpington stomped around in imperious style with an umbrella – 'What? Where do I sign, where do I sign?' She put the fear of God into me … and the Gurkhas!

Fifty Gurkhas wanted to hand their medals back to the government, who didn't want to accept them. We gave them to Nick Clegg instead. The Gurkhas cried. They don't normally do that.

The lawyers of Howe & Co. played a crucial part in the campaign. David and Martin Howe, Kieran O'Rourke and David Enright are all in our happy throng on Gurkha victory day.

Just moments after the Home Secretary says it's all over. With Joanna and Dhan Gurung in Old Palace Yard opposite the House of Commons – we were there so often it felt like our spiritual home. If ever there was a moment of joy...

Arrivals hall, Kathmandu. I attempted humour – 'Not coming on holiday again with you – can't get the bags!' I was about to have to be very assertive with the Nepal Police. I felt a little rude, having only been there for 20 minutes!

Pressing through the arrivals hall at the airport in Tibet. She's serene ... I'm panicked.

The last day of our trip to Nepal. Joanna surrounded by a sea of children at the Maiti Nepal home.

LEFT Anuradha Koirala, founder of Maiti Nepal . Everyone from presidents to airport security staff did what she said – I was no exception.

RIGHT Radhika and her son. If ever you think life is hard, you need to hear her story.

Joanna, visibly moved by the naming of a mountain view in honour of her and her family.

Kathmandu Airport. We were unaware of the scale of the waiting crowd until we emerged from the arrivals hall.

THIRTEEN

PHIL WOOLAS
7/5/2009

———•—————

s the campaign rattled through April and May
2009, Lynne and I would often sit on our balcony at
home and think, 'Phew. That was a week. It won't
get more dramatic than that.' Home is a house
called The Puffins in the village of Peene, just outside
Folkestone, built high on the side of a hill. It is only a
mile from junction twelve of the M20, but when you're
there it feels as if you're in the remote countryside. It
has an open air balcony with fantastic views. Even in
winter, Lynne and I will sit on that balcony – our little
bit of peace and tranquillity, a real haven – and talk over
life, love and the universe.

Sitting out there, we had just such a 'Phew, we need a few normal days now...' conversation on the evening of 6 May. The next day, I set out in the morning for work in Maidstone as normal. Just a few hours later, however, Lynne took a call from the *Folkestone Herald* asking what was happening, what had 'kicked off'? I was with Joanna in London, they said – they had seen me on the TV. So much for a normal day.

I had popped out from work to have my hair cut at Studio 99 in Allington, Maidstone. I was brought up as a northern boy in the era when mixed sex hair salons were considered a bit trendy – but hey, at forty-eight I was at last able to go to them and not feel too self-conscious. The hairdresser there had recently joined the Lib Dems and was very friendly. The elderly lady having her hair set next to me wasn't friendly at all.

My mobile rang. Why do mobile phones always work themselves into the deepest recess of the most awkward pocket before they decide to ring? The more you scramble and contort yourself to reach them, particularly when you are hampered by the paraphernalia of gowns and other hairdressing equipment, the more you become aware that the wretched thing is just waiting to stop ringing. And that way, the phone wins, because you then have to go through working out who you've just missed. The hairdresser kindly withdrew as I tried to call back the 'missed call'. It was Kieran, my Lucozade-drinking, fantastically, manically eccentric lawyer friend. Kieran was so angry he could hardly get his words out. Slowly pieced it together. Unbelievably, the government had written to one of the Gurkhas who had been cited in the successful High Court challenge of September, rejecting his application to live in Britain. This was the very day after Joanna had met with the Prime Minister. It seemed at best a complete internal foul up, or at worst a sign that the government was intent on toughing this out.

My mind raced. What to do and how to do it? Kieran and I batted ideas between us with the fury of a ping-pong world final. A demonstration? Not enough time. A press conference? We'd had so many in recent days. Would the press respond? Were the public tiring of the issue?

The ping-pong rally stopped. A press conference it would have to be. But where? I made feverish calls to my contacts in Nick Clegg's office to see if we could use an office or room in the Palace of Westminster. Frustratingly, we were told we couldn't. Then I had an idea. What about trying to hire a room in Millbank Studios? This building is home to pretty much all the main political broadcasters of any note. But how to get in touch? 118118 and I was through. There followed an extremely stressful series of phone calls between me and various people in Millbank. Some thought I wanted to hire a studio to make a programme, but I eventually got through to the lady responsible for the large atrium area that served as a bar and dining room. She was fabulously friendly. 'Is it for a edding, Sir?' she asked politely. 'No,' I explained, 'it's about Gurkhas.'

What was to take place that afternoon was to become one of the defining moments of televised political drama – more of a murder than a wedding. It was to rival the famous 'Portillo Moment' when Michael Portillo, Secretary of State for Defence, lost his seat in the 1992 general election to the astonishment of just about everyone – even his Labour opponent.

By now I had escaped the hairdressers. The poor lady had had to finish the job as best she could, with the scissors snipping in short bursts as I dropped the phone from my ear for a few seconds at a time.

At last I was in the car. Being in Maidstone was adding an extra pressure. To hold any sort of press conference in London I had to leave Kent straight away. The final negotiations with the atrium manageress were completed over the car phone on the M20. Having convinced her that I wasn't a completely mad member of the public, I'd explained that I needed a space at very short notice to hold a major press conference. We haggled a fee. She started at £500 and we settled at £200.

Progressing swiftly up the M20 I made calls to my main media contacts to say that there would be a press conference in Millbank at 4.00 p.m. 'Why?' they asked – to a man and woman. Kieran and I had agreed that we should keep the reason under wraps for as long as possible. It was imperative that the government didn't quickly withdraw the letter of rejection and nullify our attempts to use their crass error of judgement to further advance our cause. All I would say was: 'Joanna Lumley will be in Millbank at 4.00 p.m. and she is angry.'

The minutes were racing by as I made my way up to London. I called Joanna. At first she was shocked, then, like us, furious. She was packing up her kitchen to make way for workmen to install a new one. The kitchen would have to wait. I had more calls from Kieran. Other Gurkhas were receiving their rejection letters. The phone was ringing constantly now – journalists from every paper and broadcaster under the sun. At least they were still interested.

Then I received a particular call. This call was the moment when I knew that we were going to win this campaign. I remember precisely where I was when it came through – on the embankment near the Walkabout Bar and the Tattershall Castle, a ship now moored on the Thames as a floating restaurant. I answered the call, which had come up as 'Unknown Number'.

A calm, cool voice said, 'Hello, this is Downing Street.'

Now, I've taken a lot of calls in my life, but this was only the second ever from Downing Street. This must surely mean that our long campaign was at last getting through to where it mattered.

'Hello,' I said.

'Is that Peter Carroll?'

'Yes,' I replied.

'Hello, Mr Carroll, this is Simon King calling. I am the Prime Minister's secretary. I understand that Ms Lumley is about to hold a press conference as she is concerned that some Gurkha applications have been rejected...'

There then followed a conversation that would have been totally at home in the script of *Yes Minister*. Mr King explained to me that the letters of rejection were not *actually* letters of rejection. I challenged him, pointing out that they started off by saying, 'With regret, we write to inform you that your application has been rejected...' To my layman's eyes this seemed a pretty definite rejection. Mr King then made a pleasant, gentle but fairly desperate attempt to see if we might abort the now imminent press conference. I made a judgement call. No. We would go ahead.

By now I had arrived at the underground car park on Abingdon Street, directly outside the Palace of Westminster. The minutes were ticking by. As I strode out of the car park, I found Joanna and we made our way to Millbank. A horde of journalists walked with us, pressing all the time for comment. We kept 'mum' and arrived in the huge central staircase of Millbank studios. The world's press had assembled as agreed in the atrium below us, but the drama of the day was about to take an unexpected turn right there on that staircase.

Kieran and the other lawyers had also arrived. They, Joanna and I were on the first landing explaining to various journalists about the letters of rejection.

David Enright had brought with him some A4-size photographs of the rejected Gurkhas, some showing the terrible injuries that they had suffered serving as part of the British Army. Even John Pienaar had made an appearance.

One of the BBC journalists called me over to say, 'Did you know that the Immigration Minister is in the building?'

How things turn on such small remarks – just as that lady in Cranbrook High Street (Annie Watsham) had suggested to me in a brief conversation a few months before that I should get Joanna involved, now here was another few words that were to play a crucial role in the campaign.

'No,' I replied, 'but I do now.'

I imparted this unexpected news to Joanna. Within minutes, Mr Woolas appeared on the next landing. He looked down, saw us and, with what appeared a dismissive gesture, said something along the lines of 'I'm sure the campaigners will be happy with what I have to say' as he swept past.

Joanna and I exchanged looks. I recall suggesting she should follow him. And then the spectacle unfolded.

Though I am sure that he didn't mean to, it looked to me that the minister started to hurry towards the BBC studios and the refuge they would offer. Joanna had now started to ascend the steps in hot pursuit. She called out after him, politely as ever, but in a way that suggested he should stop and talk. He didn't. By now,

I think he had accelerated to the quickest pace one could go without actually running.

The BBC studio doors closed securely behind the minister and his two aides. Refuge at last. But at this point one of my favourite characters in this epic campaign played an absolute blinder.

Paul Lambert is one of the most experienced of the BBC's political journalists. He usually wore a brown overcoat and would often be seen smoking. He has the air of a knowing eagle and many a time he would guide us on how a press event might come across best. 'I'm only suggesting,' he would say, 'but this will look best if Joanna stands here...' And he'd point to where he had marked a spot with tape. We pretty much always took his advice.

The minister and his aides had claimed sanctuary in the BBC studios. Joanna was heading for the doors. And, bless him, Paul said, 'I can get you in...' – which he duly did. In strode Joanna, the lawyers and me, Sky, Channel 4 and a whole gaggle of print journalists. It was pandemonium. The hard-working BBC staff were standing up and using their phones and cameras to capture the scene. Suddenly, the main BBC political studios that were so used to reporting on political stories had become the story.

A very cross, very agitated lady came out of her office – I guess she was 'The Boss' – and said: 'Get out – this is a studio not a circus.' Then she saw Joanna, who had taken on the look of the Queen of Narnia, and lost her nerve.

At this point I had one of those 'Oh my God, what have we started here?' moments. The film crews from the non-BBC stations refused to leave, saying – in pretty forceful terms – that it would be unfair if only BBC journalists were allowed to cover what was rapidly becoming a major news story. We were already live on the BBC News Channel. When I went outside to explain to the now quite large throng of journalists who hadn't quite managed to tailgate through into the BBC studios what was happening, I suddenly found that I was live on TV as well. Then, the final signal that this was serious, the heavily bespectacled Nick Robinson arrived with a devilish grin that got wider and wider as he began to take in what was happening.

Meanwhile, Joanna was hovering outside the small kiosk in which Phil Woolas was being interviewed. Seeing that she was anxious to hear what he was saying, the BBC supplied a pair of headphones for Joanna. In order that I could hear as well, Joanna lifted up one of the earphones and we literally 'put our heads together' to prepare for what was to come. When he finally emerged from the studio Mr Woolas agreed to meet with Joanna and the lawyers in a private room.

By this time, I was definitely having an 'Oh my God, what have we started here?' moment. Like so many aspiring politicians I'd been on some media training days. Suddenly, I was in a position of having to handle an angry and highly mobile press pack. As the months went on, this was to become more and more my role. However, today was getting a bit much. Some journalists were furious that they couldn't gain access to the meeting now underway; others, in the atrium below, were totally oblivious to the goings on in the BBC studio but were getting mightily stressed that it was now 4.40 p.m. and the promised 4.00 p.m. press conference hadn't even started. Our campaign was dealing with the big boys of the media and in a pretty fast-moving, unpredictable and probably unprecedented scene.

Eventually, the private meeting broke up and Joanna emerged with a slightly cowed minister. I remember thinking of his two aides – both of whom looked like rabbits trapped in the headlights – why on earth didn't you get him out of this?

I stopped Joanna and Mr Woolas before they emerged from the main BBC studio and explained to the minister that we would now be going ahead with our press conference. For some reason unbeknownst to me, I asked him if he would like to join us. I was absolutely certain that he would, quite sensibly, decline. I felt sure that his aides would take this opportunity to remind him that he had a pressing meeting he simply couldn't miss.

To my astonishment, the minister said, 'Yes – that would be fine.' Fine? I thought to myself – minister, surely you don't mean that. Even though my entire media training ran to about three days, I could sense that this might not be the right call for Mr Woolas. And so Joanna and the minister proceeded down the steps to the atrium and to the waiting TV cameras and microphones.

As we gathered at the foot of the staircase, Joanna wasn't sure exactly where the diminutive Phil Woolas was standing, and when she started to speak she realised that it might be more valuable for the assembled media throng if Mr Woolas was actually visible. In a clipped tone, reminiscent of a frosty headmistress, Joanna asked where he was and when she finally located him, she ordered him, 'Here.' I'm sure she actually meant to be helpful, merely guiding him to a suitable empty space on the marble steps. Unfortunately, to many gathered there it sounded a little like the call an impatient dog owner might give to their charge. Mr Woolas duly made his way to the spot. Over the next twenty minutes Joanna employed a whole series of glares and frosty stares whilst taking Mr Woolas through their previous discussions in the BBC studio.

Throughout Joanna's speech, Mr Woolas stood with his head bowed slightly, nodding occasionally. Joanna appeared to pause sometimes and wait for one of the nods to come. He had the look of a schoolboy trying to work out how much trouble he was in. Joanna spoke softly and slowly, each phrase chosen with supreme skill. Word by word, she manoeuvred Mr Woolas into publicly restating the substance of their earlier meeting in this most public of forums.

Our team had gathered in a semi-circle behind the central duo of Phil Woolas and Joanna. The press were arrayed before us in a great arc, lights and lenses

everywhere. The room was like a natural amphitheatre. It had the feeling of a crucible. So much of modern
politics is carefully stage-managed. Most politicians
only ever engage with the media when briefed to the
eyeballs and even then they are usually guarded by spin
doctors. This was live theatre compared to recorded
television. It was raw, unpredictable and dangerous to
reputations. For the assembled media it was thrilling.

This press conference was the most memorable and
high profile of the entire campaign. It was undoubtedly uncomfortable for Mr Woolas. For many, it will
be a defining or perhaps *the* defining moment of his
political career. Such was the rawness and intensity of
the moment that some of my Lib Dem colleagues who
had come across from the House to witness proceedings felt that we may have pushed the government too
hard. They thought that it might prove to be a 'press
conference too far'. I could understand their concern.
However, on balance, I think it played a positive,
indeed pivotal, part in the campaign. I felt a twinge of
pain for Mr Woolas as he, in my opinion quite bravely,
took the heat, but then I thought of the real victims
in this issue. The Gurkhas were brave and they were
loyal, and my conscience was clear.

FOURTEEN

TEARS AND FISH 'N' CHIPS
20/5/2009

O ur campaign was focused on helping veterans who
had retired before 1997. However, the Gurkhas are
still part of the modern army and at the end of May
2009 we were all to feel first-hand the grief and
suffering that they still face as part of our armed forces.

Coporal Kumar Purja Pun was killed by a suicide
bomber in Helmand Province, Afghanistan, on 7 May
2009. At the time of his death, our campaign was at
its height. The Gurkha story was splashed across the
national media on a daily basis. We had never met
Corporal Pun, but there were requests from a number
of retired Gurkhas that Joanna might visit his family.
I remember that Joanna and I spoke at length about

the pros and cons of this situation. This was a personal tragedy of devastating proportions. The lawyers, Lynne and I talked it through many times. We didn't want to offend Corporal Pun's family by not visiting them if it were their wish. However, we didn't want to be seen to be trying to use this family's grief in any way to attract more coverage or momentum for the campaign.

I was to receive a call about this matter from a most surprising source. I had 'gone north' for a couple of days on business. One of Lynne's school friends lived up in Wakefield near my Barnsley depot. As we got on well, I had offered to take Sarah and her son Patrick out for dinner in a quaint country pub in the middle of nowhere. It was a lovely place – log fires and sleeping Labradors. The phone rang. Not unusual in itself, but when I answered the lady was particularly anxious to make sure that she was indeed talking to Peter Carroll. Once reassured that it was indeed me speaking, she told me that she was phoning from the central switchboard of 10 Downing Street. Sarah and Patrick were a bit surprised as they listened to my end of the conversation and watched me write down the number for Downing Street on a paper napkin. The lady informed me that David Hayes, Colonel of the Brigade of Gurkhas, wanted to talk to me. He had heard that Joanna might be planning to visit Corporal Pun's family.

I had a sixth sense stirring in me and I knew that I had to call Colonel Hayes. I knew that what he had to say would be very interesting. I had worked out many months before that there was a significant body of opinion in the highest levels of the Ministry of Defence that was implacably opposed to our campaign. This was never overtly stated. It just oozed out of the establishment. It was clear to me that their view was that we were being emotional, sentimental, that we hadn't thought it through and that we didn't understand, and that the Gurkhas wouldn't be able to cope here anyway. I may be being a little harsh, but it felt patronising and vaguely offensive to me. Surely, by the twenty-first century we would understand that this group, all too often referred to as 'Gurkhas', should be thought of as human beings above all else.

The only time that I was ever to have a direct conversation on this point with a senior member of the MoD was during a meeting held at the MoD building in Whitehall with a senior representative of the Home Office present. This meeting took place only after the government had finally agreed to let the Gurkhas into Britain. Joanna and I had been invited in so that these senior officials could explain what they were planning to do to ensure that measures and preparations were in place to help the anticipated increased numbers of Gurkhas coming into Britain.

We were guided through the inner sanctums and corridors of the vast Whitehall building. Heads turned as the staff realised that the defences had been breached by Joanna Lumley. Blimey ... she was actually in the building that housed the very people that had worked so hard to thwart our campaign. Eventually, we were shown into a utilitarian office. The officials were as warm and friendly as you could expect them to be when having to talk terms with the enemy. Our conversation focused on the very worthy steps the government were putting in place to make sure that the transition to the new regime of allowing Gurkhas into Britain worked as smoothly as possible. There were to be new publications available in Nepal explaining to Gurkha veterans what life would be like here in Britain. It was felt that there was a need to counter any feeling that the streets in Britain were in any way paved with gold. Everything that was described sounded admirable. However, the most interesting part of the conversation didn't involve these provisions. Unusually, the MoD representative present, I'll call her 'M' to protect her identity if that doesn't sound too James Bondish, opened up a little and talked about the Gurkha Justice campaign from her point of view. She told us that she and her colleagues had watched it with fascination. Most intriguingly, she revealed that she and others within the ministry had really questioned their stance. They'd soul searched – were they right to oppose it? They'd actually challenged their perspective. Suddenly, M snapped back into 'official' mode and I was left wondering just what conclusions they had come to.

When I spoke to Colonel Hayes he asked if it was true that Joanna was going to visit Coporal Pun's widow and family. I said that this was likely. He explained that the family were in a state of great distress and that the MoD were doing everything they could to protect them from media intrusion. He was drawing the obvious link that a visit from Joanna would undoubtedly attract media interest. I countered that we would only undertake this visit on the basis that it was kept away from the media. I, and Joanna, could genuinely see that a sudden rush of media attention would not be in the family's best interest. However, I couldn't completely get out of my mind that here was a senior officer of the British Army quite rightly and correctly trying to protect the family of one of his fallen men from further distress, whilst at the same time being part of an establishment that so often seemed to think it quite acceptable to exclude Gurkha heroes from Britain. The conversation was proper but slightly tense. If Colonel Hayes harboured any ill will towards our campaign he hid it well. The dialogue was exchanged like a considered game of chess. Each of us spoke, waited for the reply and then responded, totally unable to get a feeling for what the other person actually thought – at least that's how it felt from my side.

After much reflection, we decided that Joanna should not go to Corporal Pun's house at that time. Instead, my wife Lynne and Martin Howe of Howe & Co. went. However, a few weeks later, when the immediacy of the death had slightly subsided, we did finally visit with Joanna.

We drove up to Connaught Barracks near Dover and found the Married Quarters. Married Quarter estates are known as 'patches'. These patches have a certain 'look' – the houses somehow seem a bit lonely. I think the fact that people are always coming and going, that no one ever stays for long, result in the subtle signs that give this look. The gardens are never that well-tended. The transient nature of service life gives no incentive for gardens to be modelled by their owners. The chain-link fences that so often divide them just look military. Even when you see Married Quarters that have been sold off to civilians and have been subject to every kind of addition and customisation imaginable, they never really shake off that look.

We were greeted by a kindly if somewhat exhausted military press officer who was keeping lonely guard outside Corporal Pun's quarter. He knew we were coming and guided us into the house. There were people everywhere. The kitchen was jammed with ladies preparing food and drink. The men folk were in the hallway, on the stairs, upstairs and even outside at the back. Some of the elderly relatives that had flown over were upstairs and one was ill in bed.

Joanna handled the distress of Corporal Pun's widow wonderfully well. She was loving and gentle. I have always found situations where great depth and strength of emotion are involved very difficult to cope with. Since I've been with Lynne, I've found it a lot easier than it was, but it's still hard for me to know what to say and how to say it. I end up feeling wooden and resort to a poor version of 'stiff upper lip'.

Being in that house was deeply upsetting. This was the direct result of war. The result of valour, bravery and service. We try to protect ourselves from this horror in many ways – the pomp and ceremony of parades mask it slightly. But however you look at it, the unavoidable reality of military action, no matter how laudable and necessary the aims are, is that people get killed and families are shattered.

What on earth do you say? How do you look a grieving widow – so incredibly young – in the eye? Her anguish was absolute. And the young children – for me, the children, who understandably couldn't truly appreciate what had happened, made it all so much harder to witness. They were so full of life yet the air was so full of sorrow. All those words that tumble so effortlessly from our lips about loyalty, commitment and sacrifice crystallised in that scene.

Corporal Pun's mother and father were upstairs. His father was clearly very unwell and had taken to bed. Even in this most distressing of times Corporal Pun's family were in the terrible position of having to worry about visas and how long they might be able to stay in the UK – even his widow.

To see this pool of grief, right here, right now, was a stark reminder of why we had to win. Here was a vivid, unnerving example in our modern age of the sacrifices that Gurkha soldiers have made for Britain for nearly 200 years. The grief and suffering in that house on that day was no different from the grief and suffering behind the hundreds of thousands of Gurkha casualties across the decades. The 1997 cut-off for settlement rights was downright offensive when seen in this context.

The visit affected everyone heavily. We left the grieving family and set off for London, stopping briefly at our home for a short break. We needed to return to London promptly as the Immigration Minister, Phil Woolas MP, had asked for a meeting so that he could give us the government's latest position. Joanna had suggested her home as a quiet and secure venue.

I was dropped off at Joanna's house to ensure that someone was there should the minister arrive early. Joanna and Lynne drove on to the local fish and chip shop to collect the food. I had joked with Joanna about whether she could actually drive an Audi. She dismissively reminded me that she had driven far more demanding cars as a Bond Girl, but to my satisfaction she now managed to catch the kerb with a rather shattering clang as they shot off.

With the food collected, we gathered to receive the minister. The fish and chips were warming in the oven. The pre-dinner drinks had been served. There was concern about what the minister would say. By now, we had been joined by Martin Howe. Together, we bounced about ideas on what might be said and how we should react to each possible version. What would we say if there was an offer that might let more Gurkhas in from the pre-1997 group, but not all, as we had fought for? How would we react if the government said that all pre-1997 Gurkhas could apply, but they would only be let in at a certain rate, similar to a yearly quota system? We had the impression that the government may have yielded some, possibly a lot of, ground. However, we feared that they might be about to suggest a cap on the numbers of retired Gurkhas allowed into Britain.

Mr Woolas arrived in casual style with his colleague Jonathon Sedgewick from the UK Borders Agency. Pleasantries were exchanged. I felt like a rottweiler on a leash – eager to find out what the decision was, only to be constrained by the good manners required in such circumstances. Eventually, I could hold back no more and simply said, 'Minister – where are we?'

We were stunned to hear him quietly, and in a voice devoid of all drama, say that the government would announce tomorrow that we had won. Not in part, but totally. He even added that the government was keen to work with us to make sure that there were no unforeseen difficulties that might escalate into a substantial problem.

Martin used the opportunity to enquire into any possible cap on the numbers that might want to come to Britain and on other matters of important detail. At first, it sounded as if this was the direction that the government was moving in. Then the notion was quickly dispelled, with discussion moving on to letting all retired Gurkhas with four or more years' service into the UK – exactly what we had campaigned for. It was almost as if the idea had been floated in the hope that it would find a welcoming reception and so let the government off the hook.

As time moved on, everyone involved seemed to relax. Mr Woolas gave us an insight into the campaign from the government's side. He confirmed that all the MPs' post bags were bursting with letters on this issue and that his was particularly full. As the drink flowed, the minister opened up still more, even giving us his view of why Mr Gorbachev was the sexiest man in politics... But maybe those stories are best told elsewhere.

Once the minister had left, Joanna, Martin, Lynne and I exchanged gleeful congratulations then just sat for a while. I lay on a sofa, just drinking in the feeling of victory – it felt lovely.

FIFTEEN

DOWNING STREET
21/5/2009

———◆———

I wandered out of the back door of Joanna's beautiful, tall and elegant London home, down the few steps and into the secluded walled garden at the back. My wife Lynne and I had stayed overnight in the flat at the top of the house following the 'fish and chips with champagne' supper. Today definitely had the feeling of 'I'm going to savour this day and remember it'. This was THE day. The day that Joanna, the lawyers and I had been invited to 10 Downing Street, the day that victory was to be announced. As I walked up the garden to the annex in which Joanna and her husband held meetings, the whole mad experience of what had become the Gurkha Justice campaign flew through my mind. The first tentative steps way back in 2004 leading all the way to this – a visit to the Prime Minister to be told that our campaign, after all the setbacks, had actually prevailed.

The music room annex had previously been some sort of printing factory and latterly a taxi maintenance facility. The building had that feeling of permanence and calmness that I think comes from having a previous life. Now it was home to a large open space used for meetings, social gatherings and music. Joanna was in the small kitchen at one end of the music space. Dressed in a brown dressing gown, she was making tea and toast.

'Jam, Peter? Tea or coffee?'

Such was the normality of the conversation on this, for me, the most un-normal of days.

'I've ordered a cab for Downing Street,' Joanna said. 'Better just check on it.'

As ever in the campaign, things then took a faintly comic and ridiculous turn. The taxi didn't show. Joanna was pretty miffed about it and gave her very pointed view to the person on the other end of the phone that fouling up a taxi booking to Downing Street of all places really wasn't cool.

What to do? Time was running away from us. We had to be there at 8.45 a.m.

I suggested that we went by car. Lynne bravely volunteered to drive and with handbags and other paraphernalia thrown into the car we set off. The traffic was diabolical. The time was ticking away and away and away.

'God,' I thought, 'this could only happen to us.'

By the time we edged our way onto Westminster Bridge we had reached crisis point. Like the standard 'mad dash' scene in films like *Four Weddings and a Funeral* or *Notting Hill*, I turned to Joanna and said:

'We're going to have to leg it.'

We burst out of the car mid-way across the bridge and ran hell-for-leather past Big Ben then right up Whitehall, breathlessly excusing ourselves as we bumped into any number of stalwart commuters plodding their way to work. Several people seemed a little astonished to have had such a high speed brush with a running Joanna. I could imagine several 'You'll never guess who I bumped into today...' conversations when they finally got home that night.

We met up with Martin Howe at the black gates that now protect Downing Street, and the three of us walked arm in arm the short distance to Number 10. Immediately, we could hear the cries of the press pack gathered opposite that famous shiny door.

I had stood on that doorstep many times in this campaign. We had handed in letters and petitions and even medals. Never had I crossed its threshold. Joanna knocked on the door and it swung open. I resisted the temptation to say something jokey to the attendant, like 'Oh, you're letting us in this time' – not the right moment for jest I felt.

It was like walking into a stately home. We were greeted with the utmost charm by the very person, Simon King, who had made that rather bizarre call to me about the letters of rejection that weren't really letters of rejection. We climbed the staircase lined with photographs of previous Prime Ministers and were shown into the White Drawing Room. Joanna was beaming. If it were possible to transmit sheer unbridled happiness, she was doing it now. Throughout the campaign I had seen her, first-hand, use her voice and facial expression with studied brilliance. As Phil Woolas could bear testament, she did angry pretty well. Today, however, was just total joy.

We sipped tea and exchanged small talk with members of the staff. Then Simon asked Martin and me to leave the Drawing Room as the Prime Minister wanted to speak with Joanna on a one-to-one basis. Martin and I stood outside. It seemed a little odd to be excluded from that conversation. However, in the eyes of the Prime Minister and his team, this was very much Joanna's campaign. It was she who had confounded the political experts. We had used her celebrity status very effectively – she was absolutely identified with the issue.

The arrival of Gordon Brown was preceded by a whole host of very smart looking people. They all talked in faintly hushed tones. Then the Prime Minister arrived. Like most people, my impression of Gordon Brown had been gained by watching him on the news. How different he is in 'real life'. Tall and assured, he had a presence about him that simply doesn't come through in the media. He and his entourage passed Martin and me and entered the room where he was to speak with Joanna.

In the meantime, the staff of Downing Street very kindly showed Martin and me around the building. As someone so interested in all things political, I found the whole experience of actually being inside fascinating. We peered into the Cabinet Room. In line with custom, the Prime Minister's chair was set slightly back and turned to face the door. If a place could ooze history then surely this would be that place. So many of the great characters of British politics had sat and worked in these rooms. Decisions of almost unimaginable magnitude had been taken here. It felt like a film set, but it made the hairs on the back of my neck rise when I took in the fact that this was the real thing. Set against the enormity of the events shaped within these walls our campaign would warrant barely a footnote. Nonetheless, we were here and the campaign had been won. What better way to be told than in this special place?

A member of Mr Brown's team introduced herself, informing us she was involved in the Prime Minister's media management. Martin and I suggested to her that the Prime Minister might like to have some photographs with a joyful Joanna and the grateful Gurkhas. To our joint astonishment, this idea was met with the most lukewarm of responses. The lady indicated that perhaps the Home Office might like some pictures instead. Martin and I both pressed harder but eventually gave up. We later raised the point with Simon as well. By whatever means, the powers that be eventually agreed that there should be a garden party later that day to serve as a photo opportunity.

When the Prime Minister emerged from his meeting with Joanna he very graciously came over to Martin and me, shook our hands and congratulated us on the campaign. The man had a warmth about him that was totally at odds with his media portrayal. We had all suspected that the press would paint his decision as a u-turn or a climb-down, so I felt moved to say, 'Prime Minister, whatever the press say, you have done the right thing by these heroes today and we all thank you for it.'

He seemed genuinely touched by this and was equally cordial when he acknowledged how well we had run our campaign. I joked, 'Well, we are available for hire,' to which he gave the humorous riposte, 'Well I could do with a bit of that.'

This most important of meetings over, Joanna, Martin and I floated down the grand staircase and made our way towards the door. It swept open to reveal a mass of excited journalists eager to hear news of what had happened, what had been said and what had been promised. I think my smile was so wide that if it grew any more it would have resulted in the top of my head not being attached to my body. Maintaining slightly more composure, Joanna repeatedly explained to the insistent questioning of the press that we couldn't confirm the decision until it had been announced by the Home Secretary in Parliament later that day.

Some of our party returned to the Churchill Café on Whitehall, the opposite side of the road to Downing Street. We were trying manfully to avoid doing any interviews, as we had given our word to the government not to. I made one exception and spoke with John Warnett on BBC Radio Kent. John is widely regarded as the 'Voice of Kent' and I always felt that he had a special affinity with the Gurkhas. Like mine, I think his father had passed on stories of their valour and service.

As the time of the announcement drew near, we gathered one more time in Old Palace Yard directly opposite the Palace of Westminster, as we had done on so many occasions. For us, Old Palace Yard had been the scene of anger, disappointment and jubilation. In a sense, it was the spiritual home of our campaign.

The formal announcement was to be made by Jacqui Smith, the Home Secretary, just after twelve noon. Martin and Joanna were at the front of the assembled mêlée. I stood a few rows back with an odd sense of detachment. One of the media crews had given Joanna a small hand-held radio device so that she and we could hear the Home Secretary make the formal announcement. Even though we knew what was coming, I had a strange feeling of nervous apprehension. It seemed to take hours, rather than minutes, for the Home Secretary to get to the key part of her statement and to make the announcement. Then it finally came. The words themselves said so much more to me than that the Gurkhas could now live in Britain. They were bringing to an end the monumental effort of so many people. They were the culmination of all the thinking, the plotting, the brainstorming, the small coincidences and chance conversations, the marching, the petitioning, the media work, the ups, the downs, the sheer bloody-minded determination, the luck and the madness of it all. I heard those words of victory through a deep calm, like watching a goal being scored at a football match as a bystander rather than a supporter. The scene itself conveyed something to me of the importance of it all. Here we were again in Old Palace Yard with the Palace of Westminster stretching out wide across our view, bathed in bright sunlight. A thousand Gurkhas were joyful and tearful. Joanna punched the air.

We all said some words. In my few, I tried to make sure that the assembled media understood that this campaign had relied on the support of hundreds of thousands of people who had all contributed to its sense of momentum in some way, and that so much of this victory was down to them.

<hr />

Later in the day, Downing Street made contact with us about the possibility of getting thirty retired Gurkhas to attend a brief 'tea in the garden' with the Prime Minister at around 4.00 p.m. News of this event spread amongst the assembled Gurkha throng. Completely unintentionally, confusion was to reign.

Downing Street is protected by high black gates. I understand that they were put in to protect Downing Street during the time that Margaret Thatcher was

Prime Minister. I can recall going on a day trip to London in the 1960s with Mum and Dad when the security at Downing Street was very different – there were no barriers and I could go and actually stand, nervously, on the steps of Number 10. How different it is now. The gates themselves are quite formidable. After them comes a security ramp that rises out of the road, which, I imagine, is designed to stop car and truck bombs. All visitors are screened by police and have to go through body scanners, with any bags passing through airport-style X-ray machines. As well as all of this, there are quite a number of heavily armed police officers. It was against this background of intense security that our Gurkha Garden Party was about to unfold.

For those of us at the centre of the campaigning effort, today had been an emotional experience to treasure. For the retired Gurkha community, the day was even more significant. For them, this result was nothing short of life changing. It meant that hundreds of retired Gurkhas who were living in the UK with no proper status, always worrying that their latest appeal to stay may be rejected with the resultant threat of the 'knock at the door' from the deportation squad, could now properly live here with their families. There would also be several thousand retired Gurkhas back in Nepal who would now be able to see a new and more hopeful future in Britain.

All the retired Gurkhas with us that day had served with our army, some for many years. For them,

Downing Street had huge symbolism. Many simply couldn't believe that they were actually standing on that street – let alone that they would be going into Number 10 as the personal guest of a serving Prime Minister who had just sanctioned a decision that would change their lives.

Shortly before 4.00 p.m. I introduced myself to the armed police guard at the gate of Downing Street and persuaded them to let in thirty retired Gurkhas.

Then another thirty, I understand nominated by Kieran, showed up. The police on the gate were very unsure about letting these other thirty in. This was stressful, to say the least. And it was to get much more so when even more Gurkhas appeared, and I mean many, many more. Clearly, in the jubilation of the moment the small detail that only thirty retired Gurkhas should go to the event in the back garden of Number 10 had been lost. I was inside the gates, looking out back through them to Whitehall, and what I could see was a large number of retired Gurkhas who had thought they would be able to go in and were now confronted with the reality that they couldn't. In the end, I had to vouch for all the Gurkhas and we ended up with about 150 calmly and patiently waiting just inside the security gate at the top of the street.

At this point, a very stern lady in grey appeared from inside Number 10 and strode up to the assembled throng. She picked me out and said, 'I am responsible for the security of Number 10. Can I remind you that this is the home of the Prime Minister and one of the most security sensitive establishments in the UK? Can you tell me what's going on here?'

Not for the first time in this campaign I so wanted to speak the truth and say something like, 'No, not really – because I don't know myself.'

I thought that such a blatant show of total honestly might completely blow the day, however. In a fairly desperate attempt to go for the 'Please don't be cross with me, I'm well intentioned here and I don't know what I am doing' technique, I asked Joanna to come over in the hope that the lady might soften in her presence – no such luck.

'One hundred and twenty of these people have to leave,' said the very stern lady.

'Oh my God,' I thought.

This was not a good moment. Here was a lady asking me to tell 120 of the joyful retired Gurkhas who had actually got past security at the end of Downing Street that they had to about face and leave, while thirty of their comrades got to go on in to the event.

I looked pleadingly at the policeman with the machine gun who had wandered over to see what all the fuss was about. Alas, it was to get worse.

At this juncture, another policeman pointed to the securely closed black gate. Standing there was a man replete with kilt and bagpipes explaining in the most earnest terms to yet another policeman that he was part of our campaign. Having been in the campaign since the start this was news to me, but the policeman insisted that I come over and talk to him nonetheless.

With a completely straight face, the man explained that he regularly played the bagpipes on Westminster Bridge and that he'd 'bumped into' one of our lawyers about an hour ago in the pub. As a result of that brief meeting, he thought that he should be allowed in. The lady in grey was watching this scene develop and giving me a look that said quite clearly 'And I'm supposed to take you seriously?'

Having explained to the police that the man just wasn't with us and under no circumstances could I vouch for him, I went back to the task of trying to persuade the very stern lady that all the Gurkhas should be allowed in. I explained as best I could that trying to select 30 from the 150 would be a fraught process on its own. How on earth would you pick who was going to stay and take part in the event and who must be asked to leave? Every single one was a British Army veteran and each had as much right to be there as any other. And even if we could make that difficult decision, the logistics of getting that many disappointed people back out of the street onto Whitehall would be a mammoth undertaking.

In the end, I pretty much just begged for mercy and Joanna turned on the 'Lumley Charm'. To my immense relief, the lady in grey couldn't resist the cocktail of Joanna's charisma and my 'little boy lost' look and relented. I think she too had been moved by the whole Gurkha story. What a relief.

The throng of retired Gurkhas all went through security and formed an orderly, if somewhat longer than expected, queue on the footpath on the opposite side to Number 10. Then the great black door was opened and in they filed. All at Downing Street were fabulously kind, but slightly taken aback by the numbers – as were we. The veterans were escorted into the Cabinet Room as the staff lined the route through the building, many applauding. And finally we spilled out into the garden of Number 10.

The Gurkhas milled around the garden. It felt like a summer tea party in the days of empire. The staff was hastily trying to source more cups and saucers. David Enright was keeping watch for the emergence of the Prime Minister and when Mr Brown and his wife Sarah came out, David announced him with great style, in his booming oratorical voice, as 'our Prime Minister and Prime Minister of the Gurkhas'. Mr Brown mingled and greeted the throng. Jacqui Smith and Phil Woolas were both there. Everything about the event was just lovely and wonderful.

Mr Brown made a speech warmly welcoming the Gurkhas and acknowledging the strength of the campaign. Joanna was gracious with her reply and made the point that history would pass a kind judgement on Mr Brown for his brave decision to give all retired Gurkhas the right of settlement. Here were the very Gurkhas who had been denied legal status in Britain, many for years, sipping tea with the highest elected politician in the land. The scene was magical. You almost had to pinch yourself to prove that it was really happening. For me, this was the most significant part of Victory Day – to see these fabulous retired Gurkhas not just standing outside Parliament, but inside the garden of Number 10 was a compelling image. The Gurkhas weren't just coming – they had arrived.

SIXTEEN

NEPAL
25/7/2009

———•———

The visit to Nepal was planned before we even knew that we would win the campaign. At first it was to be a small-scale private trip – Joanna, Dhan Gurung, Lynne and me. Our aim was to visit the Gurkha veterans in their homeland and tell them that we would fight on for their right to settle. But as the campaign grew, so did the visit. Joanna wondered if her husband and son could join the group. Then the lawyers came aboard, closely followed by their families. And once we had finally won, interest in the trip completely exploded. The media interest reached truly stratospheric levels. ITV wanted to come along. Then the BBC. Then Sky. Then the *Daily Express*, *The Sun*, *The Times*, *The Mirror*, AFP, Nepali TV...

For some local journalists this would quite simply be the reporting trip of a lifetime and they were absolutely determined to make sure they were on that plane. The group was made up of Sarah Saffi of the *Folkestone Herald*, Chris Denham of the *Kent Messenger*, Ed Cook of BBC Radio Kent and Mark Norman of BBC TV South East Today. These were journalists who had started covering this cause when it was still relatively small. They had followed us through the good times and bad, from the early marches to the steps of Downing Street, and they wanted to see it through to the end.

Ed Cook had reported on the evolving story for years on the airwaves in the campaign's home county. Ed has a deep, rich voice – in the nicest way, he really does have a voice fit for radio. After the many, many radio interviews that I gave or listened to during the course of the campaign, radio voices have become a source of great fascination to me. The only time I've heard a voice of a similar calibre to Ed's and actually been able to meet the person behind it was on a campaign-related visit to BBC Television Centre early one morning. I was there to do the *Today* programme and I just happened to be in the studio when Rory Morrison read the news. His was the distinctive voice I heard reading the news every day and here he was, reading it now, in ever such a measured way. It's easy to imagine that if Rory were faced with reporting the end of the world, you'd be able to rest safe in the knowledge that every beat of his phrasing would be completely unperturbed. His description of death and destruction would flow out like syrup from the tin and he'd still finish absolutely on time to usher in *The Archers*. The only disappointing thing about Rory Morrison was that he was wearing jeans and a jumper – somehow that just didn't seem right. I'm told that in Lord Reith's day, radio presenters would sit behind microphones as big as suitcases wearing their dinner jackets. Perhaps that was over the top, but should a Radio 4 newsreader, with a voice that almost *is* the news, wear jeans?

I was to learn that Ed had received a string of awards in the world of radio journalism and during his trip with us to Nepal I caught a glimpse of why he had been so lauded. Ed can seem rather diffident when not 'on the radio'. He has a disarming hesitant manner, almost overly polite. Then suddenly, when recording or interviewing or reporting, he becomes almost like another person – assured and confident, delivering velvet voice radio. I was to tease him gently that he has the broadcast equivalent of a 'telephone voice'.

Ed and Mark Norman both worked very hard to keep a steady stream of live and pre-recorded packages coming back to their teams in Kent. The UK–Nepal time difference was significant, so it very often meant that they would be setting up their equipment to do a 'live' broadcast just as we had all finished dinner and were about to retire. On at least one occasion I did a live interview from Ed's hotel bedroom. He had a very strange device that looked like a tea tray, which we had to point into the sky to try and locate some distant satellite signal. I understand that later in the visit Ed had to actually go up onto the hotel roof when he needed to make reports.

The *Kent Messenger*'s Chris Denham appeared at Heathrow for our Nepal trip replete with Crocodile Dundee hat and backpack. He even had the half-consumed bottle of water always at hand that is the key piece of equipment for any seasoned traveller. Chris had endeared himself to Lynne and me by his stalwart contribution at our major media events. We soon decided that he didn't lack confidence when at work... During one of our big events, the presentation of a petition bearing 240,000 signatures at Downing Street, the media pack that had gathered was enormous and bordering on the ill-tempered. Handing in petitions at Number 10 was a tool that we used several times during the campaign. The petitions themselves, by their very nature, carried a message, but the act of presentation was almost more important since it was something that the media could film and photograph, helping us keep the issue high on the media agenda. So there are Joanna, Martin Howe and I standing with a small group of retired Gurkhas and our twelve sacks of petition forms on the steps of Downing Street. This was the sort of event at which Joanna's celebrity status really bore fruit. I've been to petition Downing Street on smaller campaigns and I've pretty much had to ask the policeman if he'd mind taking a picture. Not so with Joanna around. There were dozens of film crews

and photographers, all shouting out different instruc-
tions. 'Look this way', 'look that way', 'just Joanna on
her own please', 'Joanna can you put your hand on the
wheelchair' – and so on, and on, and on. Eventually,
little Chris Denham sat down in the middle of Downing
Street and appointed himself Master of Media. Bear in
mind that Chris was a local reporter who would often
have to take the pictures to go with his story. And here
he was laying down the law to photographers who
looked like they could eat him for breakfast.

The last of our intrepid band, Sarah Saffi, worked on
the *Folkestone Herald* under the editorship of Simon
Finlay. Simon had arrived in Shepway at almost the
same time as I had done in 2000. I had come to take up
my post as the new prospective parliamentary candidate for the Liberal Democrats in Folkestone & Hythe.
Simon was set to work on the *Kent Messenger,* but he
soon moved over to the *Herald* and took the helm as
editor there. Simon had a very keen interest in all things
relating to the politics of the Shepway (the name manu-
factured by an act of local government for the area that
would be so much better named Folkestone, Hythe and
Romney Marsh) and he could be quite harsh, always
keen to dig into a story and make life a bit uncomfortable for the local politicians. Some would say that he
could be 'over the top' in this regard; others would say
he was just being challenging. Heaven knows, my experience of the extraordinary world of local democracy
has left me in no doubt that it needs a profound shake
up. In the meantime, a little bit of 'roughing up' by the

local paper is truly welcomed by those of us who find the pomposity of so many local councillors suffocating. Sarah was from the same paper, but of a different journalistic stable from her editor. She was gentler, more anxious to get a fair and balanced view of a situation, and she seemed sincerely moved by the story of the campaign itself and particularly by our trip to Nepal.

I believe that the majority of these journalists were prepared to pay their own way on the Nepal trip and I really admired their commitment. I think that some were able to get at least some contribution from their papers and stations in the end. Nonetheless, even before this was offered they had decided to come. Both Lynne and I were immensely moved that they felt such a strong tie to the cause that they would come along at their own expense.

I have always had a keen interest in everything to do with politics, including the various state occasions that are the backdrop to all of our lives. When you watch a head of state or a senior politician arrive at a major event, even from the comfort of your own home on the TV, you get a real feel for the scale on which the press and a million other factors have to be carefully managed. Cars arrive and leave, high-profile figures climb in and out, the screen fills with the multiple reflections of a thousand camera flashes – and behind the scenes there are people looking after the luggage and the travel documentation; people fussing and worrying about the schedule; personal protection, almost unseen, keeping a watchful eye on proceedings.

The logistics of these occasions require immense planning and attention to detail – usually undertaken by a large team of professionals. Now, suddenly, what had started as a small campaign team outing had become something more akin to the affairs of state I had observed from my sofa. But this was a private trip. There was no team of professionals – all the planning was down to us, and a large part of it purely to me.

Fortunately for all of us, I received significant and much appreciated help from the UK Defence Attaché in Kathmandu, Colonel Jeremy Ellis. Colonel Ellis had contacted me, in the most tactful way possible, whilst I was still back in the UK planning the expedition. Throughout the weeks leading up to the visit, he offered me advice and support by email and phone. He did this with the greatest of sensitivity, though on occasions I sensed that his very traditional British reserve was forcing him to hold back what he really wanted to say. I know he had serious doubts that we fully understood the logistical challenges that the climate and the poor communication infrastructure would present, but he made sure never to let his feelings show.

Colonel Ellis was supported in his diplomatic attempts by the retired Colonel William Shuttlewood of the Gurkha Welfare Trust (GWT). The GWT is a charity based in Salisbury, established some forty years ago, that raises money to help support Gurkhas in need, principally back in Nepal. My understanding is that the majority of the GWT's funds come from a wide spread of individual donors. Some give money as a straightforward donation. Others do things to raise money – sponsored walks and cycles, expeditions and the like. In addition, the Ministry of Defence makes a substantial contribution to the coffers each year. Perhaps it is for this reason that the charity seems to have an almost martial feel to it. My time in the RAF was a short but invigorating six years and, despite its brevity, military service had almost burnt itself into my psyche. There is something about the way that particular environment feels – its mark remains on people and places, long after the military has moved on. So it is with the GWT. It is not a military organisation, it is a charity. However, the armed forces' influence pervades it. William Shuttlewood, delightful as he could be, still had the air of an army colonel. If I closed my eyes at meetings with him and his team, I could drift back to the days of my service. I could so easily have been at a military briefing.

I am certain that the retired Gurkha officers working for the Gurkha Welfare Trust and the staff at our Embassy in Nepal were more than a little concerned that the trip would end in disaster. Between them, Colonels Ellis and Shuttlewood tried to warn me not just of the practical challenges our group would face, but also of the personal perils we would each encounter. I can't remember which one of them ordered me to keep my mouth shut in the shower, but I was assured that the bugs in the water were so virulent and plentiful that even a splash of cascading water whilst 'rub and dubbing' in the shower could induce serious infection. At first, I was sceptical. But since this story was corroborated by other reliable sources, I made sure to always shower with my mouth tightly closed. It is actually a lot more difficult than it seems. Likewise, cleaning teeth – the temptation to just rinse that toothbrush under the running tap before putting it back in your mouth for a final scrub is enormous. My faith in the advice of the two colonels was to be completely affirmed, however, when one of the journalists on our trip suffered a lapse of concentration, sipped a glass of water and, within hours, was in intensive care with serious internal bleeding caused by a water-borne bug. From that day on my lips were sealed so completely in the shower that I swear I nearly passed out through lack of oxygen.

Even with the wealth of expertise offered by the two colonels, the logistics of the trip still looked and felt horrendous. Bhim, one of the original four Gurkhas from that first fateful visit to my home, seemed to take a great pleasure in telling me just how bad the roads would be. The first problem would be the potholes. Some were allegedly as big as bomb craters. And if we could navigate safely round them, it was highly likely we would find ourselves behind one of the hundreds of very slow rickshaws, or other 'vehicles' that would be doing no more than 20mph. Then there would be cows. Cows are sacred in Nepal. They have right of way and no amount of frustration can get around it. After that, there was the risk of heavy rainfall, which could rapidly transform the road into a mud bath. Finally, assuming that we survived all of these road trip nightmares, there was always a chance that a monsoon could trigger deadly mudslides. Suddenly the delays on the M25 didn't sound too bad by comparison.

So how to resolve this? Bhim suggested that his brother might be able to 'borrow' a couple of military helicopters – apparently the Nepalese Army still uses some old Russian-built choppers that were passed to them after the Cold War. 'Is that how it works over there, Bhim? We borrow them?' This felt like a bad idea right from the start. I am no expert on aviation safety, but I was definitely not happy with risking life and limb – let alone Joanna Lumley – in an ancient, war-ravaged helicopter, particularly one that was 'borrowed'. Just to be certain, I floated the idea with Colonel Ellis during one of our many telephone calls. The moment I mentioned this 'helicopter option', there was a classic British army officer silent pause, which clearly said 'That's not an option I'd recommend' without him saying a word.

Military aircraft rejected, I decided to focus on the marginally more sane option of trying to charter some planes. These would be proper aircraft from a proper airline, I said to myself – as if this was an entirely everyday occurrence for me. As if, when running a medium-sized transport company in Larkfield, I had frequent reason to hire aeroplanes. Suddenly, I was not only media manager and tour operator, I was travel agent as well. Of course, I would be able to charter planes to fly us around a foreign country. Why wouldn't I? Now where on earth was I to start...?

As ever, try Google. After a few non-starters, I finally found Buddha Air and managed to get through to a wonderfully helpful lady by email. Some of the correspondence must have been deeply unsettling from her point of view. Here I was sending emails asking if I could charter Buddha Air's planes, but I didn't actually know where I wanted to go or when I wanted to go there. I didn't even know how many seats I needed. Then, there was the question of how to pay for these planes. Wisely from their point of view, Buddha Air wanted payment in advance. But how on earth was I to sort that out? No problem, I hear you say, just use a credit card. Have you ever tried to use a credit card to hire aircraft in Nepal? My word, that was a challenge. And when you add to all that the fact that the number of journalists who wanted to come was going up and down like a yo-yo, you might get a feel for what an administrative minefield this had become. One TV crew only wanted to come on our flights if they could actually be on the same plane as Joanna. They wanted to do one of those 'in the air' shots of her reflecting on the trip. I had to do some ducking and diving to make this happen. I explained to Joanna that she might now have to travel in a second plane – 'You've sold me,' I recall her saying.

On more than one occasion the stress of the planning, the total uncertainty of the details and the sheer scope of the endeavour all got me to the point of wanting to screw up the tens of thousands of printed emails from hotels and Buddha Air, scream at the top of my voice and bin the whole venture. But I didn't – I couldn't. It was going to be the trip of a lifetime. For all of us.

SATURDAY 25 JULY 2009

The total number of people involved in the 'Royal Tour' of Nepal had reached forty. In all, the party that was scheduled to meet at Heathrow for our flight out numbered ten. There was Lynne and me, Joanna, her husband Stephen Barlow and her son Jamie, and Dhan Gurung would also fly with us. Then there were the local journalists – Ed Cook and Mark Norman of BBC South East, Sara Saffi of the *Folkestone Herald* and Chris Denham of the *Kent Messenger*. Geraint Vincent of ITN also showed up, but he was flying first class. The lawyers and their families were already out in India on holiday and so would fly in to meet us there. Alastair Leithhead of BBC Far East would fly to Nepal direct from Thailand. Sky was sending a team from the Middle East. Various news agencies were despatching people from cities all around the region. And journalists and photographers from a whole raft of national newspapers were making their own way there. Many had flown out in advance so that they could cover our arrival.

The Air India team that met us at Heathrow were wonderfully friendly, allowing us to use their first-class lounge. Lovely though that was, what I really wanted them to do was to allow us to use their first class seats! During the hours preceding the flight I launched a new campaign – Campaign Upgrade. I hinted and suggested and explained, but all to no avail.

Those few hours in the VIP lounge were lovely. This was to be one of the few times that we would all gather outside of the 'fighting' part of the campaign. It was genuinely lovely to be able to relax and talk safe in the knowledge that there was no march about to start, no petition to deliver and no plot to hatch. The lovely atmosphere was only disrupted by the completely unasked for input of a couple of boorish MPs who were on our flight on unrelated business. They were concerned about the 'unintended consequences' of the campaign. I just hoped that they'd clear off and sit somewhere else. Joanna was, of course, entirely Joanna-like – serene and pleasant.

The hour of departure came and we boarded the plane. My campaign for an upgrade had enjoyed limited success – the captain instructed his crew to escort Joanna and her family to the first-class seats, but it was economy for the rest of us. We settled into our seats for the long flight. What lay ahead we did not know. As the plane taxied around on the runway, I watched the TV monitor ahead of me, which was showing the view from a camera on the nose wheel looking straight ahead.

We started moving faster now along the runway. The engines went quiet for a second, and then steadily built up to the take-off roar. The runway lights began to flash past on the flickering TV monitor, gathering speed. The bumping sensation quickened and then disappeared as the jet lifted off. Nepal, here we come.

SUNDAY 26 JULY 2009

Since there were no direct flights from the UK to Kathmandu, we had to change at Delhi. This was quite an experience. Major city airports look very much the same the world over – lots of glass, moving walkways and adverts for 'top end' goods and services that I suspect very few passengers could ever afford. Delhi was no different. What was different was the attitude of the staff.

Those of us en route to Nepal were escorted from the Heathrow flight and made to stand in a line. A man in a military uniform relieved us of our passports and then proceeded to call out our names as a classroom teacher might have done in the 1930s. 'Carroll, Peter,' he barked. I hadn't had this since my days at RAF College Cranwell. 'Lumley, Joanna.' The whole group burst into laughter. 'Yes, Sir!' she burst out, just as Goldie Hawn would have done in *Private Benjamin*.

The flight from Delhi to Nepal took about an hour and a half. Eventually, we landed in Kathmandu, our party now swelled by the lawyers, who had met us in Delhi, and we stretched and yawned our way back into life as the plane came to a stop. We waited impatiently to be allowed to disembark. You know the scene: the seatbelt sign isn't yet turned off, but already the aisle is crammed full and everyone is contortedly trying to reach out and up to get their belongings out of the overhead lockers. Kieran switched his mobile back on and read out a message from someone who was waiting to greet us in arrivals. It seemed that for some reason they had experienced incredible difficulties getting to the airport. I distinctly remember thinking that this must have been due to some security incident, or that maybe it had been caused by famous road chaos in Nepal.

Finally we were off the plane and met, right there on the tarmac, by our old friends Madan Kumar Gurung and his wife Meena. Seeing them here, in Kathmandu, was an emotional moment. They had spent many months living in England in that grey world of inter-mediate legal status under the old immigration rules, not daring to go back to Kathmandu for fear of being denied entry should they then have attempted to return to the UK. Now they were free.

We were also introduced to the woman who would become the real star of this visit and our godsend through all the logistical difficulties – Dhan's auntie, Anuradha Koirala. This tiny but powerful woman had an innate air of authority that meant everyone in Nepal took her seriously. She was to act as our main point of communication, arrange trips, assemble convoys of cars for us and generally make things go smoothly.

Together our group moved into the big open space of the terminal building. Slightly disconcertingly, at this point men wearing surgical masks were taking people's temperatures as part of a precautionary screening for bird flu. They pointed some kind of thermometer at us. Heaven knows what would have happened if we had been 'hot'. Would they have sent the unfortunate 'hotties' back? Fortunately we didn't have to find out!

All felt calm and well as we were processed for visas and our passports were checked. The hall was almost silent. Then, this last stage of airport procedure complete, we walked towards the doors that led into the main public area of airport arrival and pushed them open.

Immediately, a mass of media surged forward and Joanna was surrounded by a swarm of people. An over-enthusiastic Gurkha leader reached forward, put his arm around Joanna and pulled her away from us, further into the midst of the crowd. Suddenly the situation was alarming. People piled into the expanding gap between her and me. All at once I knew that I could no longer be just a member of the successful Gurkha Justice team – I had to be Joanna Lumley's bodyguard. I had to physically pull Joanna back. Unbelievably, the police were just looking on. It felt rude but I had to make the point pretty firmly that they needed to do something – like stop us getting crushed to death. The noise was deafening – people shouting, clamouring, the commotion of hundreds of bodies moving simultaneously. There were camera flashes everywhere. Kieran and Martin were battling to try and keep a clear zone around Joanna. For most of the journey from the arrivals door to the waiting car, we weren't really in control of the direction in which we were travelling – we were caught up in a tide of movement. Martin and I ended up with our arms locked around Joanna in a protective ring. I was overwhelmed by a feeling of panic.

What I most wanted to be able to do was to look around, identify the person who was supposed to be in charge and ask them to sort it. No chance in this mêlée. What to do? How to get control? How to make sure that Joanna was safe? I pulled myself up to my full height and, summoning my best RAF parade square voice, thundered: 'Get back. We are not moving until it is safe.' I ordered a group of Nepali policemen to form a line in front of us, giving us a chance of getting through – not very polite of me, perhaps, having only just arrived, but needs must.

Struggling to strike a light-hearted mood I whispered into Joanna's ear, 'I'm not coming on holiday with you again – too difficult to get the bags.' In all honesty, I really was terribly concerned that this was going to go wrong, and badly wrong at that. We were exhausted from the long flight, suffering the inherent difficulties of coordinating forty people in a country that most of us had never been to and suddenly we were confronted by scenes we could never have imagined. The Nepali media were frightening – pushing, shoving and shouting. Behind them, waiting calmly, were thousands of retired Gurkhas and their families. In the brief moments when the veterans could get to us through the offending Nepali media, we were all struck by their warmth and generosity. I tried hard to be gracious in the face of the warmth of their welcome, whilst still maintaining control as best I could in that enormous sea of humanity. By now, Joanna and I were drowning in a sea of yellow khadas, a type of ceremonial scarf, and garlands of real flowers. One lady managed to come up behind us and put a khada round my neck from behind – as the crowd pushed us forward, I got caught in a scary moment of potential strangulation.

As we swam through the crowd, Anuradha, our salvation and guide, suggested we push left to our waiting car. At the same time, Dhan was telling us to swim the other way. By now, Alastair Leithhead of the BBC was on the scene and he simply launched himself over the top of the crowd – like a surf boarder throwing himself into the sea. Chaotic doesn't quite cover it. We were used to large-scale media coverage in the campaign but this was just overwhelming.

All of a sudden, one of the police officers forming the protective line moving before us fell over in front of me. I could see the newspaper headlines back in the UK in my mind's eye: 'Joanna Lumley dies in airport crush – Peter Carroll blamed.' It really was all hell and no notion now. I fought to try to stay upright as the mass surged. By now the headline running across my vision read: 'Beloved Joanna Lumley killed – unknown Lib Dem councillor definitely to blame.'

How we all remained standing I'll never know, but finally the police swung into action, employing a pretty simple but effective technique. They hit a lot of people with sticks. Whilst this was clearly wrong and unpleasant and offended my liberal principles, it did at least allow us a fighting chance to make it to the car. As I held back the adoring crowd, Joanna, who throughout all of this was sublimely serene, mounted the running board of the car to make a short speech. Then, at last, we were in the vehicle. We had arrived in Kathmandu.

This reception was the most extraordinary that I have ever been part of. The fact that a small part of it was for me felt wonderful but almost unreal. Though it was close to terrifying for those of us in the midst of it, for those merely observing the joyous, if somewhat chaotic, scenes, I can imagine that it looked and sounded wonderful. This was why some retired veterans couldn't get to the airport – there were just so many people already there.

We drove away from the madness of the airport to our hotel, The Dwarika. This was to become our oasis in what would prove to be an overwhelming week. The Dwarika was constructed out of reclaimed buildings from Old Kathmandu. Its rooms were lovely – vast and beautifully designed. Outside, the chaotic madness of Kathmandu could rage, but inside all was serene.

MONDAY 27 JULY 2009
Our first full day in Kathmandu was spent visiting the Foreign Minister, the Prime Minister and the

President before addressing one major rally of veterans in City Hall, and another at a nearby hotel.

That morning was to be the first real test of our logistics. Auntie and her team were remarkable. They had assembled a whole convoy of vehicles to ferry us around, including minibuses to carry the media. The vehicles were already lined up inside the covered walkway of the hotel reception. We all climbed aboard and set off into the streets of Kathmandu.

Chaotic and manic were the words that sprang to mind. The traffic was dense and fast-moving. There appeared to be no rules at all. People went round roundabouts in both directions and there was lots of hooting and tooting, but despite the disorder there was no real aggression – Dhan told me that 'road rage' was almost unheard of in Nepal. However, on the downside, it was not unheard of for people with no sight to be given a driving licence. Our convoy snaked through the city, one minute on wide roads, the next on barely cobbled narrow cut-throughs. It was raining – hard and torrential. In places, the drains simply could not cope and our tyres made bow waves as we passed.

The roadsides teemed with daily commerce. We passed a shop selling CDs and records only to see a cow sitting quite happily in the middle of it, no doubt enjoying its 'sacred' status. Some of the establishments were extremely humble. Only a few items of food or produce graced their unglazed windows and their owners sat on the steps giving off an air of resignation, waiting for the next sale. Despite all the worries racing through my mind – getting to where we needed to be on time, what would happen next and how would we get through this incredibly tight schedule – I was able to take a few seconds to savour the feeling of this new place. The colours, the sounds, the smells – all were so very different from home.

Nepal is a struggling country. It is desperately poor, ravaged by democratic uncertainty and still appears to be trying to find a sense of itself politically. In all our visits to its government departments we were treated with the greatest respect and courtesy, but for me the physical surroundings revealed so much about the country's financial woes. We waited for the Foreign Secretary in a room populated with armchairs that in the West would have been passed on to less well-off relations. There was no sense of pomp or grandeur as there would be in London or Paris. However, this did not detract from our appreciation of the sincere welcome we were being accorded by the highest levels of Nepalese society, and Anuradha organised it all with the aplomb of a discreet master of ceremonies.

The Foreign Minister duly arrived. Sujata Koirala had actually visited Lynne and me in our Folkestone home many months before – indeed, the day of her visit was just before our victory in the High Court in the September of 2008 – so it was a warm welcome, and affectionate words were exchanged.

We then moved on to meet the Prime Minister, the aptly named Mr Nepal. The Nepali press were keen to get a picture of Joanna and the Prime Minister exchanging gifts. So keen were they, in fact, that their pushing and shoving reached unanticipated new heights. Mercifully, on this occasion we were separated from them by a coffee table. This may not seem like much, but that table had the single virtue of being at just the right height so that as the journalists pressed against it with their shins, the natural physics of the situation meant that they fell across it, whilst another layer of photographers fell, in turn, on top of them. I could vividly hear Chris Denham of the *Kent Messenger* shouting out words of remonstration from the back of the room about this behaviour, but all to no avail.

Before leaving for Nepal, a most enterprising Kent County Council officer had visited me at work in Maidstone to ask if I might try and make use of the Nepal trip to help the county. He had primed me to ask if the Prime Minister might pass on to the relevant authorities an offer from the council for Kent to be their base for pre-Olympics 2012 training. This I duly did, presenting the Prime Minister with a pack of information, and I believe that Joanna said something that was interpreted as an invitation for the team to stay at her home in south-west London during the games – at least, that was how it was reported in the London press.

The Foreign Minister and Prime Minister's reception completed, it was time to meet the President. We were shown into what looked like the Nepali equivalent of the Cabinet Room at Number 10 and waited in hushed silence for the President to come in. The tables formed a giant square, with our group seated around three sides, and the fourth at the top being reserved for the President. I sat close to the top table next to Joanna. 'I've never met a President before...' I said. 'Pete, nothing to worry about, I have... Usually American,' replied Joanna calmly. Ah well, we all move in different circles. When he arrived, we found that the President's serious manner masked quite a sense of humour. He greeted Joanna with a wry smile, saying, 'I wish I could get as much media coverage in Nepal as you.'

These meetings were truly wonderful experiences. I'll probably never again in my life have a day in which I meet a Foreign Secretary, a Prime Minister and a President, one after the other. That said, such encounters are very much 'events', constrained as they are by the shortness of the appointment and the need to adhere to protocol and procedure. There was no feeling of meeting the person; rather, we met the office. With this in mind, I was already looking forward to meeting the Gurkha veterans, to putting names and faces and expressions to this group of heroes that had been the whole raison d'être of the campaign.

We were soon to get that chance.

Our first introduction to the Gurkha veterans of Nepal took place later that day at Kathmandu City Hall. The steps outside the building were full of expectant veterans and their families. Our convoy drove in through the main vehicle entrance and made its way to a side door leading into the great hall. This door led, in turn, to a narrow corridor, which was packed with Gurkha wives dressed in shimmering bright green saris, all carrying flowers and garlands. We pressed our way down the corridor and emerged just in front of the auditorium's central stage. Thousands of joyful faces looked down on us from the steeply banked seating. The warmth of their applause seemed almost tangible, so vivid with emotion that you could physically touch it. The camera flashes and the piercing glare of the lights atop the TV and video cameras only added to the sense of drama.

The scale and warmth of the welcome as we walked out of the entrance tunnel into the main body of the hall will live with me forever. We were greeted by a cacophony of sound, full of love. I felt as I imagine an England footballer would feel upon emerging from the players' tunnel at Wembley. In the terms of our campaign, this was our World Cup winners' ceremony.

And at that moment I experienced what was for me one of the highlights of the entire campaign. As we made our way through the crush to the stage, one particular Gurkha made an obvious effort to reach me in the crowd. He took my hand. 'Thank you, Peter' – that was all he said.

Kieran whispered in my ear that this was Gyanendra Rai, the Falklands War veteran whose back had been blown open by a piece of Argentinean shrapnel and whose life was saved in the Port Stanley field hospital by Naval Surgeon Commander Rick Jolly. As a result of his injuries, Rai was retired from the army and all his subsequent attempts to come to Britain had been refused. He was often cited in our campaign as an example of how outrageously immoral and unfair British government policy was on this issue, and he was even mentioned in the Commons debate that led to the defeat of Gordon Brown.

For this quiet, dignified man to say 'Thank you' to me felt overwhelming. It meant more than all the praise that was heaped upon the campaign. This was real. This was personal. This was the physical manifestation of what the campaign had achieved. Even now, writing these words, the recollection of that moment sends a shiver down my spine. Who would have thought whilst he lay fighting for his life in that bitter conflict that I and my colleagues would play a part in his life all these years later.

Walking onwards, we found ourselves showered with gifts of scarves, plaques, certificates and knives. The presentations came thick and fast. And as I moved to the front of the stage to address the crowd in their rows and rows of precipitous seating, it felt like I was addressing a wall of people. I always knew that this campaign had right on its side – but now I could both see and feel that. We were later to learn that some of those people staring back at us had walked not for hours, but for days to be there. It was deeply moving and utterly awe-inspiring.

That first day was punishing. The heat and humidity were oppressive. But our confidence in the various logistical arrangements had received a great boost – Auntie Anuradha had been superb.

There was one last crucial challenge left, however. It had been agreed that we would have tea with the British Ambassador at 3.00 p.m. in his residence. In this tight schedule of intense diplomatic-style visits to dignitaries galore, this was the one for which I was determined beyond all rationality to be on time. This would be my way of saying, without words of course, that we (or I) were capable of doing this kind of thing.

In the face of the traffic, the rain, the sheer size of our convoy and the inevitable delays, we arrived at the British Ambassador's residence with military promptness, at 1455hrs for our 1500hrs function. Colonel Ellis managed a brief acknowledgement of the enormity of our achievement as our convoy moved through into the secure compound. Despite the scale of the campaign we had organised, and the huge significance that it had for so many people, this small detail – actually arriving on time – felt like a real coup.

I imagine very few people get the opportunity to have tea with one of our ambassadors in a far-flung, exotic corner of the world. I have to say, it's quite a revelation.

The building would have been quite at home in Surrey – large spacious rooms set in extensive manicured gardens; light, bright and easy. Staff were on hand to serve tea from elegant teapots and cake cut into precise, military segments. A clock ticked gently in the background. I had thought that the days of the Empire had passed. Not so. We could have been a hundred years in the past. It might have been a set from one of those old British films in which our brave officers had gone to quell some rebellion in some far-off land.

Then there was the ambassador – charming, affable, thoroughly British, he would have been quite at home in a Bond film. Cigar in hand, 'our man in Kathmandu' was wonderfully understated. I half expected Judy Dench to come into that reception as 'M'. We were to share a day with him later in the week in the west of Nepal, when he accompanied us on a visit to find out how the Gurkha Welfare Scheme (GWS) uses the charitable funding raised by the GWT back in the UK.

There was one moment of typical Britishness during our visit. We had arrived as a complete team, including the lawyers and all their families. The Embassy was only expecting about eight people and there just wasn't room. Now, if that had happened at my home in Folkestone, I'd just say: 'Well, let's find some extra cups and all muck in.' Not so in ambassadorial circles. No, we had to decide which eight could go in – and the others, well, they just had to go and fiddle around somewhere else.

Lynne generously volunteered to solve the problem by going shopping with Jamie, Joanna's son. His luggage had failed to arrive, so he was mostly wearing my clothes. As any self-respecting man would, I felt a little sorry for Jamie as Auntie Anuradha and Lynne took him into Kathmandu to buy clothes. Anuradha probably didn't help when she took the opportunity, just at the moment that Jamie was in his underwear, to point out to the locals that this man was the son of the goddess on the front page of the newspaper they were reading.

While the others 'kicked their heels', the ambassador had arranged for Joanna to lay a wreath at a simple memorial that lies in the grounds of the residence. I looked on from the sidelines. It was hard to keep hold of the fact that this was an entirely private visit – this impromptu ceremony had all the trappings of a state occasion. The photographers were held back behind a rope and there were military guards who snapped to attention as the ambassador and Joanna solemnly approached the memorial.

With this latest hurdle successfully cleared, we were scheduled to move on to another gathering of older veterans in a nearby hotel, hosted by the Regimental Associations. Though our confidence had grown, we hadn't yet reached the point at which the stress of constantly having to think what was supposed to be happening next had disappeared, and the heat, the humidity, the adrenalin and the jet lag were draining.

Our convoy stopped hundreds of yards short of the building. The weaving line of retired Gurkhas and their families stretched all the way from there to the room at the hotel that had been booked for the event. As we made our way along the line we received flowers and garlands in abundance. Many people held up simple signs offering thanks to Joanna, to me and to Howe & Co.

Speeches were duly made and Joanna conducted herself with perfect poise throughout the proceedings. But her emotions were soon to be brought to a trembling head. A frail, very elderly man pushed his way through the throng at the front of the room. In the cacophony and chaos, he enlisted others to get word forward that he had a special reason to actually speak with Joanna. Those around him heard his plea and helped him forward. Suddenly, his motive became clear: here was a man who had served with Major James Lumley. Here in the flesh and blood, wizened and frail though he was, was a direct link to her father. The emotion was searing. Just as Joanna's meeting with Tul Bahadar Pun had done, this encounter brought home the undeniable connection between past and present, and drew together every thread of the entire campaign. The ITN cameraman fought to gain a position from which he could film this moment. The whole focus of the room was on his and her clasping hands. Sixty-five years shrank to nothing.

With this final emotive surge added to the fatigue of the day, I realised I was completely shattered. We returned to The Dwarika, every single one of us exhausted. The evening was filled with organising Joanna's various media engagements and then, at last, some food and sleep.

The psychological rollercoaster of this visit was well underway.

TUESDAY 28 JULY 2009

The next day we flew out east to Jhapa and then on to Dharan. My extensive negotiations with Pryanka from Buddha Air had proved, against all the odds imposed by the distance between the UK and Nepal, successful – for this stage of the trip we had chartered two eighteen-seat planes with Buddha Air. Some of the party were nervous about flying and someone asked me what Buddha Air was like. My attempted joke that they were called Buddha Air because if you crashed you just came back in another seat wasn't well received.

The part of the airport we had seen just a few days before – the international arrivals building – had been quite impressive. It was small, but reasonably modern in its appearance. The structure that housed domestic departures was not quite so modern. It had an air of authenticity and mayhem. I was certain that, at any moment, Michael Palin would walk past. Just trying to find the plane was quite a challenge – at the appointed time, someone opened the door from the crowded lounge out onto the tarmac and vaguely waved towards a line of aircraft. When I was young getting the right bus in Mersey Square, Stockport, with Mum or Dad was always preceded by a conversation with the bus driver along the lines of 'Excuse me, is this bus going to Great Moor?' Now, here in Kathmandu, I found myself having the same kind of conversation with the plane crew.

Our confidence in Nepali aviation took a further

knock once we were safely in our seats aboard the correct plane. An elderly gentleman and his sweet grandchild boarded, looked around at all the fully occupied seats and then disembarked to go for a wander around the apron. Clearly, he had heard our flight called for Bhadrapur and thought, 'I'd like to go there.' Then just ambled onto the plane. Oh, how very different from airports in the UK.

In truth, Buddha Air was fabulous. Pryanka, who looked after all our flights, coped with everything from passenger numbers rising from four to thirty-eight, to the itinerary changing pretty much every day in the months preceding our arrival and the fact that we were late for our flights on a number of occasions.

So here we were. Two planes successfully chartered. All seats full. Our formation duly taxied and roared down the runway, and then we were in the air, heading east for Jhapa. This was a 'pinch myself' moment if ever there was one. I was in Nepal. Thirty-eight of us were airborne, including journalists from the BBC, ITN, and a host of newspapers and press agencies. How on earth had I got here?

We flew for about an hour. Conversation was muted by the sound of the twin engines so I contented myself with pressing my head against the window and watching Nepal pass by underneath. This was not the Nepal of the soaring Himalayas – beneath us were undulating hills with wisps of mist between them and then, in turn, plains stretching out as far as the eye could see.

We landed at Bhadrapur airport with its concrete runway – no problems – and taxied to the airport building. This was my kind of airport. It was no bigger than a small semi-detached house. One room was arrivals; next door was departures. The VIP lounge was a tiny box room with a curtain as a screen. The expression 'in the middle of nowhere' suddenly meant something to me. Nonetheless, despite the remoteness of the place, here was a seemingly endless line of welcoming smiling faces. This was Dhan's home area. His whole community had closed up shops, schools and farms – some to meet him at the airport, others to welcome him in his home village about an hour away by car.

As we made our way from the airport building greeting the long line of people that lay between us and our waiting cars, I was notified that our day's plans were being threatened by one of the most destructive forces at work in the retired Gurkha community – division. Dhan had organised a programme of activities, greeting, dancing, singing and speech-making in his home town. Another group of retired Gurkhas had organised a completely separate function some miles away and had sent a representative to the airport who was now trying to hector and badger Dhan into getting our party to go to their function as well.

This was completely unfair on everyone as it meant that there were now two quite separate events that we were under pressure to attend when we had thought there was only going to be one. It was unfair on Joanna – since none of us could bear to contemplate a situation where a group of retired Gurkhas would miss meeting their champion – and it was even more unfair on Dhan. His great moment as the prodigal son returning home was now threatened with being over-shadowed by our need to try, somehow, to make sure that the Gurkhas at this other event got the treatment they deserved. As it happened, the event that Dhan had organised in his home village had very few retired Gurkhas present; the majority were at the other event. Dhan was hugely distressed by this.

Nor was the situation fair on me. Trying to organ-ise this whole mad adventure was testing enough. We were trying to do too much already. The group was enormous and any error or overlap that meant we missed a flight could so easily end up with thirty-eight of us sleeping rough. To my discomfort, I had to disap-point Dhan to some extent. I insisted that we must take Joanna to the other event, even if this meant that the time spent in his home village would be reduced. He argued that the other group organisers were effec-tively trying to sabotage the programme. I agreed with him – he was quite right. But being right wasn't the overriding factor in this situation. The truth was that somewhere out there was group of Gurkha veter-ans who had been told they would see Joanna. Some of them would have walked for days to get there. To disappoint them would have been unthinkable. I was, quite frankly, bloody furious, but I conferred with Joanna and she agreed that somehow, whatever it took, we had to see this other group.

So now I had to become Sergeant Major, ordering people to get into cars and to start moving as we went through the difficult process of early departure. We rattled and hurtled along those inadequate roads and if it's possible for an entire convoy to swerve as one, we did. We had the benefit of a police escort to keep our route clear; and it was needed. I could feel the pressure of the ticking clock. I had been told in no uncertain terms that if this re-planning meant we were running late and missed the last flight of the day, we would end up completely marooned.

Eventually, we reached the village that was home to the 'other' event. Outside, under a canvas to shield them from the sun, Joanna met about eight veterans of the Second World War. All feelings of stress and anger left me. Just the look on their faces was enough to confirm for me that we had made the right decision. To have missed them would have been cruel. From there, we walked a few yards into the village hall and Joanna said the briefest of words. Then we were off, back to the airport.

The choreography of the day was now more than a little strained. We were late, but fortunately the plane had waited. We flew on to Biratnagar, the airport that serves Dharan, the great eastern city of Nepal and a long-time area for Gurkha recruits. The customary airport welcome awaited us and we set off on the long journey by road to Dharan itself.

Some miles outside the city, we became aware of a great throng of motorcycles. There were at least a hundred, many flying Gurkha flags. They had come to greet us and escort our cavalcade into Dharan. They made an incredible sight. As we wove our way through them, our local BBC man, Mark Norman, could resist no longer. Suddenly, he was out of his vehicle and riding pillion on one of the motorbikes. Hanging off the back of the bike, his body leaning sideways at a perilous angle with camera held low, he was doing what journalists call a 'piece to camera' – at speed. Here was a man in his element. When questioned about what the BBC back home might think of the Health & Safety implications, he seemed to miss the irony of his reply that what the eye didn't see the heart couldn't grieve over. More than one person observed that it would be pretty easy for the BBC to 'see', since they were going to broadcast it.

And so to the City Hall. The crowd was so large, so dense, that it felt as if I made the entire journey from car to building without my feet having touched the ground. This was one of the most raucously joyful of our receptions. There was singing and dancing in abundance. Understandably, our hosts wanted us to stay and savour the moment. But I could feel the ticking clock in my head. Time was marching on. Discreetly, I made our host aware that we simply had to go. Just getting Joanna out of the building was a real challenge. Everyone, and I mean everyone, wanted to talk to her or to give her a gift – I wanted us to catch the plane back to Kathmandu. We finally emerged from the building only for the BBC's Alastair Leithhead to collar Joanna. I burst right into his interview, not realising that he was live on the BBC News Channel. 'We're going to miss that plane' were my less-than-gracious words of interview termination.

We raced back to the airport, the minutes ticking by. I called Pryanka of Buddha Air to explain that we were running late. She was quite composed. She explained it wasn't a problem. I felt a little calmer. We hurtled on. I shared the journey back with BBC Radio Kent journalist Ed Cook. Ed had appeared to be behaving a little oddly. In a moment of light relief, we got it out of him – he'd had the misfortune to split his trousers and had been forced to walk around with a very large jacket around his waist, hanging down to cover his modesty, not a pleasant clothing arrangement in the appalling heat and humidity.

On we sped. I made a couple more calls to Pryanka at Buddha Air. Still no problem. The journey seemed to be taking an age. I called Pryanka one last time. We were now horrendously late. 'Sorry, Peter,' said the voice on the end of the phone. 'We couldn't hold the planes any longer, they had other jobs to do and we had to send them away...'

Then the line went dead – the phone lost reception, or Pryanka had just gone silent, or perhaps she'd even hung up. I am sure that many people have had mobile phone conversations that have delivered bad news. To describe your body's reaction as a sinking feeling doesn't quite cover it. I can still feel the involuntary movement of my other hand coming up to meet my drooping head. Burying my face in my hands seemed an entirely appropriate response. Then, after a few brief seconds, wonderful nectar words were suddenly sounding in my ear: '...but we have found one other bigger plane ... and it will come and get you...' Pryanka will never know just how close she brought me to cardiac arrest.

When we arrived at the airport, it was to find that Buddha Air had diverted another plane for us. But, quite spectacularly, this was no small twin-propeller craft; this was a four-engine BAE 146 – a proper plane. A jet airliner all to ourselves. I sank into my seat. Never have I been so grateful to see a plane.

Our most demanding day was over. We had flown from Kathmandu to Bhadrapur, from Bhadrapur to Biratnagar, and Biratnagar to Kathmandu. We had somehow managed to fit in a second, unexpected meeting with veterans. It was with great relief that we returned to the oasis of The Dwarika and prepared for whatever the trip was to throw at us next.

WEDNESDAY 29 JULY 2009

There is something about Nepal that makes the country special. Even now, months after returning home, I can't quite put my finger on it. This unexplained feeling of magnificence was strongest for me during our day visit to the Gurkha Welfare Scheme (GWS). The GWS is a strange mixture of servicemen and civilians who perform charitable works in Nepal to benefit Gurkhas and their communities using money raised by the long-established UK-based charity the Gurkha Welfare Trust (GWT). Though I was familiar with the GWT, I had no idea of the breadth and depth of the work they do through their 'in-the-field' arm – the GWS put in water standpipes to bring clean water into isolated villages, build bridges in remote valleys to give communities better transport links and provide medical support that is essential when so many people have to walk so far to find a hospital.

I had initially had immense reservations about taking part in this part of our tour. Indeed, Joanna, Lynne and I discussed whether I should go at some length. Right up until the last minute, the accepted wisdom was that I should not go.

My relationship with the GWT was not the easiest. Without a doubt, the GWT and the GWS do a vast amount of good work that brings relief to retired Gurkhas and their communities, and there is a very strong argument that without their help and the donations of the many thousands of people who support these charities, many retired Gurkhas would have suffered terribly.

I first met representatives of the GWT in the basement rooms of Joanna's London home. The campaign had started to repeatedly hit the headlines. We were making a lot of progress and the Gurkhas were now news. As the major charity responsible for supporting retired Gurkhas, the GWT quite rightly felt that they should understand the campaign and any implications there would be for them in the, at that time, unlikely event that it would be successful.

There was, and probably still is, a massive cultural divide in this situation. Here was the long-established GWT – a charity with strong links to the Brigade of Gurkhas and the army in general, and a track record of helping retired Gurkhas back in Nepal – suddenly confronted by a campaign addressing the very issues at the core of the GWT's remit. Our campaign was public, political (with a small 'p') and fast-moving. I was always left with the feeling that the management team of the GWT loved Joanna immensely, but was horrified that she'd been led into this business by that odd chap from Folkestone who was always making a fuss and being a damn nuisance.

They were incredibly nervous of me. I suggested that they should meet the lawyers. This sent them into a veritable spasm. I think they saw the lawyers and me as some sort of modern-day freedom fighters. At one of our meetings, this one in an army club just off Pall Mall, Colonel William Shuttlewood, then the effective head of the GWT, asked Joanna and me, 'But who exactly are you? What is the constitution of your campaign? Who funds you? Who are your members? What is your remit?'

I answered him. 'It's me – I started it – Joanna and a bunch of Irish human rights lawyers, plus most of the country. We have received very little funding. Our aim is to win. We have no formal structure. We are not intimidated by the odds.'

It looked like he simply couldn't compute. 'What?' I could hear him thinking, 'No constitution, no structure ... no formal remit.' Worse, he was probably thinking, 'and you're causing all this mayhem on the Gurkha issue ... which might have an untold impact on our world ... and there are only a handful of you.'

In another meeting, I asked Colonel Shuttlewood to meet some of the Gurkha veterans who were fighting with us in the campaign. Bravely, he said he would do this and I convened a meeting in a small café opposite the Institute of Directors in Pall Mall. I say bravely because I suspected that for him this was stepping out of his comfort zone. Here was a retired senior British Army officer, now running a very conservative (with a small 'c') charity, meeting with 'other ranks' (the retired Gurkhas involved in the meeting were all from the ranks). He was listening to their concerns and problems, which, in turn, related to the very issues underpinning a campaign that was both extremely public and political. At that meeting, he heard first-hand that British Army Gurkhas who had retired before 1997 were suffering here in Britain. The law forbade them to work. They could claim no benefits, not that they wanted them. Some were ill and struggling to get basic medical cover. Most were sleeping on floors or sofas. All were desperately short of money.

Eventually, I brokered a meeting where the lawyers did meet with the GWT. It all felt a bit uneasy. The trust appeared very concerned about what they called the 'legal issue'. They worried that if they gave assistance to these men, they would be condoning an illegal act because many of the retired Gurkhas' legal statuses were 'vague'. This didn't sit well with me. Here was a charity that had been established to help retired Gurkhas arguing over a point of law before giving desperate men some help. I am aware of the argument that the charity had a responsibility to uphold the law. However, most of the Gurkhas in the UK were in some form of protracted appeal process and therefore it could reasonably be assumed that they had grounds to remain here until the appeal was either granted or denied.

I always thought that the GWT could have done more at that stage simply by diverting some of their financial clout into the local groups that were supporting Gurkhas. It's worth pointing out that the majority of retired Gurkhas had been obliged to contribute to the GWT during their service. This was supposed to be their charity as much as anyone else's. Sometimes, it felt to me as if this was, in fact, the MoD's charity. However, on the more positive side, the GWT did appear to grasp that it would have to consider changing how it worked in the event that our campaign was successful and large numbers of older retired Gurkhas did come to Britain.

We often felt that the GWT and many of the people associated with it thought that the country was doing enough for the retired Gurkhas purely by virtue of the work being done by their own charity. The guiding philosophy of all we were doing in the campaign was that retired Gurkhas had a right to fair and equal treatment in relation to UK service personnel. A large part of our argument was that it shouldn't be covered as 'charity' – a great amount of what the GWT supported should instead be covered as a national responsibility.

For example, there are about 5,000 very elderly retired Gurkhas living back in Nepal who are veterans of the Second World War. Many of these men are living in absolute poverty. They are reliant on a charitable monthly payment of about £30 a month from the GWT. This handout is called a 'welfare pension', though in reality, it is not a pension. There is an argument that the cost of living in Nepal is very much lower than it is here in the UK. A bus driver in Nepal might be lucky to earn £300 a month. However, even taking this lower wage level into account, that £30 a month only just keeps these veterans from abject poverty. Can that be right?

When we had returned from Nepal, I watched the thirty-minute documentary that Alastair Leithhead produced about the Nepal trip – Joanna Goddess of the Gurkhas. I believe that it was transmitted on the BBC News Channel but not on the main BBC stations. I was horrified to see a clip near the end of the film that showed that Joanna and I had missed an elderly veteran who was anxious to talk with us about his circumstances. He had been caught in the open by a Japanese fighter plane in the last days of the war. He had been hit several times. He had lost his foot and was blind in one eye. And he was, and possibly still is, living in terrible conditions on his £30 per month charity handout. I absolutely commend the GWT for giving him that at least. But my simple question to us as a nation and to the successive governments that have represented us is this: should a man who faced that amount of suffering as a result of fighting with our ancestors be left in utter poverty, reliant on charity, however well intentioned and valuable that charity is? In my book, it's a simple answer: No.

It was against the background of this shared history that our visit to the GWS took place. The local GWT had extended such a warm invitation that I found it difficult to refuse and, in the end, our trip was truly inspiring. The day started early back at Kathmandu airport where we were to catch our charter flight to Pokhara in the west. By now, based on our experience of flying all over the east of Nepal on the preceding day, I had the confidence of an experienced travel agent. We duly boarded flight Buddha Air 605.

The day before we had flown over many miles of flat country that had looked like an outstretched quilt of patchwork squares; today's flight west took us over more mountainous terrain. Looking down, the scene was of rising hills capped by wispy plumes of cloud and mist. The plane had two lines of seats; each was nine seats long, either side of a central aisle. This layout and the noise of the propeller engines made any sort of communication very difficult, so I contented myself with just staring down at the unfolding wonder of the country below.

After about an hour, the crew began to prepare for landing. If I leaned slightly into the aisle and looked to the front, I could see right out through the cockpit window, which was fascinating. I could feel the aircraft getting lower. If I looked out of the side window I could see the tops of the hills, now much closer than they had been only a few minutes ago. The descent continued. I looked along the aisle and out through the cockpit. All I could see was mountain. No sky, no horizon, just mountain – and still we were headed right for it. Then suddenly, just when that mountain looked a lot closer than was decent, the plane banked steeply, the mountain disappeared and we headed down into Pokhara.

Colonel Ellis had also flown out and was on hand to meet us on the apron. Outside the airport, the retired Gurkhas had once again shown up in large numbers to greet us. Though they must have numbered several hundred, there wasn't the manic chaos of the initial greeting on that first day. The veterans had lined up along the edge of the central approach road to the airport and Joanna and the rest of us were showered, once again, with flowers and garlands, passing a myriad of makeshift signs of welcome and thanks. By some means, a plainclothes policewoman had appeared and was carefully walking with Joanna as a close protection officer might do for a VIP. At first, I felt a bit put out. Up until then, that responsibility had fallen to me.

Our group split. The lawyers were, perhaps understandably, not overly keen to join the main scheduled event as guests of the Gurkha Welfare Scheme and (by association) of the Gurkha Welfare Trust, so they did their own thing that day. Meanwhile, Lynne, Joanna and I were hosted by the GWS in great style. The UK's ambassador to Nepal, Dr Andrew Hall, joined us in his Land Rover Discovery, complete with satellite comms on the roof. This mode of transport fitted in quite nicely with the image of him as a James Bond-style 'our man in the East' that I had gained at our previous encounter.

Our first appointment was at the HQ of the GWS for a briefing on the extent of their medical support for retired Gurkhas, together with an insight into their work putting running water into villages. As I sat in the darkened briefing room, I was genuinely impressed by both the scope of the work and the obvious care that the staff took in delivering help and support. It came across as a matter of pride. At the end of the briefing, the GWS team explained their plans for a new initiative. For the first time, they were constructing a form of sheltered housing for some veterans. Generally, in the Nepalese culture, the elderly stay with extended family in their villages, but the first such building was now under construction on land next to the HQ.

One of the scheme's staff, Lieutenant Colonel Adrian Griffiths, told us that he had been the subject of a Maoist kidnapping some years before at the same time that Michael Palin was visiting his unit. Adrian came across as an archetypal British Army officer. He recounted his ordeal with gentle understatement. He and six others had been held against their will for over forty hours by armed men, many of whom would have been regarded at that time as terrorists, but Adrian related the whole experience as if he'd popped out to the shops and his car had broken down. His tone was one of mild irritation that he'd been delayed, with no indication of any trauma at the fact that he had been abducted. Colonel Adrian, as everyone seemed to refer to him, also explained that he would regularly walk to visit and check on those veterans living out in the remote hills and mountains of the area. Sometimes, these walks would take as long as a couple of weeks. I was genuinely moved by the degree of care and compassion that this showed. He assured me that all British Army Gurkha officers would do the same. Whatever my views on what more the government and the MoD should be doing for Gurkhas, this experience left me in no doubt that the money raised by the GWT is used well and wisely out in Nepal.

With the early morning briefing over, Joanna was able to meet some veterans who had fought with her father and then, mercifully, we took tea before getting in the convoy and heading out to see some of the work undertaken by the GWS.

Dr Hall was in his ambassadorial Bond-mobile and Joanna was his guest of honour. Lynne and I had the fun of travelling in the military attaché's Land Rover Discovery. In a joyous quirk of fabulously daft diplomatic protocol we had a flag on the front of the car. For some unknown reason the diplomatic seniority of an ambassador didn't command a flag.

The convoy snaked its way out from Pokhara. The beauty and majesty of Nepal was rapidly becoming apparent. Slowly the roads became rougher, steeper and began to twist and turn. There was the occasional small mudslide or, here and there, a stream raging directly over the road.

The Land Rovers made easy work of the ascent to Pumdi Bhumdi school. The media bus had a bit more of a struggle, and several journalists emerged shaken and stirred. Pumdi Bhumdi was a delightful experience. The staff and teachers were thrilled beyond measure that Joanna was visiting. The school had been completed with the help and support of the GWS some years before. It was not a pretty structure. Grey concrete, no glass in the windows – if it had been in England, it might have looked unfinished. But to the community here it was a treasure and an immense source of pride. The children were happy, bright and sparkling in their simple uniform. They were all the picture of beaming, shiny-faced young innocence.

The stark contrast between young people and schooling here and in the UK hit me. Many of these young people would have to walk two hours to school and then two hours home. After that, I imagine that most would have to help their parents work the family patch of earth to ensure the family's survival. There were no computers. There was no fancy technology.

But despite all that, the children were polite and disciplined, even charming. You could sense a passion to learn, a real interest and commitment. It felt a happy place to be.

Lynne started up a simple game with the dozens of children who were by now squeezed in behind us as we sat in an arc of armchairs, waiting for the formal greeting from the headmaster. 'Thumbs up,' she would chant, giving them the thumbs up sign. Then followed a jaunty 'thumbs down' sign. The language barrier was pierced and we all laughed and smiled our way through the visit.

With farewells duly said, the Joanna convoy now moved on to one of the welfare centres that the GWT/GWS support. Here, in this remote outpost at Syangja, there was no crowd. However, the few dozen veterans that had come to see Joanna had endured hours of walking and bus journeys.

Next we went out into the hills. Our destination was Chaura, a tiny hill village. Our aim was to see first-hand a newly installed fresh water system provided by the GWT/GWS. Putting water into the remote villages of Nepal changes lives – not only are there the obvious health and sanitation improvements, but there are considerable benefits not immediately apparent to the outsider. Hundreds of thousands of Gurkha women have their bodies crushed by years of having to bring water from far-off wells back to their homes. The weight of carrying heavy containers daily on hip or head literally wears them out, causing all sorts of medical problems, from back pain to serious internal injury.

The gentleman guiding me said it wasn't far – and then offered me a ski pole. The fact that I was being offered a ski pole by a Gurkha was deeply worrying. What followed proved that my worries were well founded. We walked up and up and up. Lynne was sprinting around the hillside like a mountain goat. Joanna was somehow managing to walk in serene mode and appeared to be completely unphased. I was sweating buckets. The gentle mocking laughter of my Gurkha companion wasn't helping either.

We trekked higher and higher. Lynne had stopped and was looking away from the hillside out across the valley. She seemed transfixed. I heaved myself to a panting halt next to her and we looked out together.

I cannot describe the feeling of looking out at the valley stretched before us in a way that would do it justice. It felt as if the colours and the majesty of it were literally flowing towards me, as if we were drinking in the view. It was a wonderful experience – I just stared and stared. Rapturous nearly captures the feeling. Bizarrely, for someone who had never previously ventured to these parts, it felt like home. It felt familiar, warm and comforting. It moved Lynne to tears.

We had a few brief minutes to walk through the hillside tracks that passed for village roads. The houses were of wood, with earth floors. There was no electricity. This looked and felt like a hard life. Despite the obvious poverty, however, every single person – man, woman, boy or girl – that I passed offered a gift. It might have been just a few flowers picked from the field or some leaves from a plant, the value of the gift itself was of no importance. Here, deep in this poor country, where life was tough, it was the giving itself that really mattered. We have lost so much back in the West by comparison.

That evening Madan Kumar Gurung, who Lynne and I had sheltered back in the UK during those hard months of campaigning, with his wife Meena and son Silas, hosted a dinner for all the team at the Fishtail Lodge, just outside the town. The lodge sits on an island and can only be reached by a pontoon barge that is pulled across the lake by hand. We ate and drank and relaxed with the media crews. I tried my hand at Nepalese dancing; this consists of making 'like a tree' and gently flowing and bending. Well, that was the theory. I suspect that in my case the reality looked just like bad 'dad dancing'.

The day's events over, we made our way back to the aptly named Shangri-La hotel in Pokhara. By now a monsoon was in full swing. The plants bent under the force of the deluge and the eaves of the low hotel buildings turned to waterfalls.

THURSDAY 30 JULY 2009

The struggles and sacrifices of the Gurkhas are legendary and, partly as a result of our campaign, there is now an even greater awareness of the injustices that they suffered. Having been at the centre of the campaign for some years, and having built up strong ties with many veterans, I thought that we'd seen and heard the worst of the stories. But we had not.

On Thursday morning, a group of elderly Gurkha widows had asked to visit Joanna in the hotel. They also wanted to meet the lawyers to hear from them how the recent changes and concessions to immigration might affect them. I popped in and out of the meeting in between organising various media slots and interviews.

Some of the Gurkha widows were relating their stories to Martin, Joanna and Lynne. If ever faces had misery etched on them it was the faces in this room. Even without an interpreter, you could feel the anguish in their voices – the Nepali words almost sounded like a form of beseeching. These women had been so poor, so isolated, so driven to the edge of despair that they had been forced to give away some of their children. By doing so, they had hoped to be able to feed the remainder. These were women in their sixties and seventies. Their whole demeanour, their expression, their whole aura bore witness to their terrible grief. The women in our party looked distressed, speechless at the depth of suffering being laid out before us.

We had attended major rallies in city halls in Kathmandu and Dharan in the east. We were now to go to a similar event in Pokhara. However, by this time, the desire of certain Gurkha groups to cause difficulties was extreme. Dhan Gurung had masterminded most of the programme. However, other groups were insistent in trying to hold their own events. It looked and felt like the people running some of these groups were prepared to use their veteran membership in order to get their own way. It really was very tiresome. But the last thing I could allow to happen was for Joanna to be 'embarrassed'. And so, as in Dharan, we were forced to make concessions. Dhan was almost reduced to tears by the stress of it all on more than one occasion. I really felt for him.

In Pokhara we had to go to one event knowing that we simply had to leave at a particular time in order to make sure that none of the veterans missed Joanna. I said to Joanna that at the appointed moment, which I would signal, we would have to stand up, smile a lot and leave. The moment came – just as the chief Nepali guest arrived. When he realised we were leaving, he looked mortified. People were now coming forward making a thousand pleas for us to stay. I led Joanna out as the mood turned unfriendly. We definitely caused offence here, but what can you possibly do when you are convinced that one group is deliberately trying to make you miss the other group's event?

Those of us who had been on the GWT/GWS day met up with the lawyers and their families and some of the journalists for a last drink in the bar in the cool of the evening. 'How did it go?' asked Martin. Joanna, Lynne and I all had to acknowledge that the GWT/GWS were doing more than we had thought and that what they were doing, they were doing well. Martin seemed a little dismissive of it all. A mildly fractious conversation followed that gave the end of the day a 'jolted' feeling. As the alcohol flowed, Martin's view became a little more entrenched than normal. I sensed Joanna's irritation. When agitated, she has the habit of running both her hands through her hair and flicking her head back at the same time and this happened more than a couple of times that evening. Time to retire, I thought.

FRIDAY 31 JULY 2009

We had factored one 'leisure' experience into our schedule. This was to visit Lumbini, the birthplace of Buddha. We assembled our things and arrived at the airport for the flight, only to be told that there was a slight hitch.

'Mr Peter,' said the staff member, 'we have a technical problem.'

'What's that?' I asked.

'We don't have a plane,' he said, with a completely straight face.

We all agreed that that was the best type of technical problem to have, but by now we were all exhausted, physically drained by the heat, the humidity, the jet lag, the emotion and the action-packed schedule.

Some of the media crews slumped in the armchairs of the VIP lounge. Others whiled away the hours pacing around outside the room on the concrete forecourt that merged into the apron and the runway. We were caught in a 'will the plane appear, won't the plane appear' limbo. To be honest, I suspect that most of us were so tired we were hoping that it never showed.

After some negotiation, Buddha Air kindly agreed that they would fly us back to Kathmandu, but take a detour so that we could fly alongside the Himalayas and, hopefully, see Everest.

This we duly did. There was much banter on board amongst our merry group. Kieran is not a great flyer. There were cracks in the plastic surrounds of the aircraft windows that I'm sure were purely cosmetic. However, some were taking photos of these cracks on their mobile phones and passing them to Kieran. Definitely not kind. The plane battled on to reach 25,000 feet. To our left, the mighty mountains were clearly visible and there, standing like a pyramid above all the others, was Everest. Oh the joy of flying in Nepal. One by one, the crew invited us to come to the front and lean right into the cockpit to get a wider view.

We landed for the last time in Kathmandu and filed out of what by now felt like the familiar surroundings of the airport to head back for the sanctuary of The Dwarika. To one side we could see an assembly of giant old Soviet-style military helicopters. Presumably these would be the ones that Bhim had suggested we just 'borrow' to get around. Having seen them 'in the flesh', so to speak, I'm glad we did no helicopter borrowing and stuck with Buddha Air.

That afternoon we diverted from Gurkha matters and paid a visit to Maiti Nepal, a charity based in the centre of Kathmandu.

Maiti Nepal is big. If you drove past it you would be forgiven for thinking it was an unusually attractive modern housing development, with its accommodation towers surrounding a large open central garden area. But this is no ordinary housing estate. Maiti Nepal needs to be big because it is helping a huge number of people to overcome the effects of one of the great evils of the age. It is home to literally hundreds of women and girls who have been rescued from traffickers and brothels across Nepal and India.

The charity was established and is run by none other than our very own 'Auntie' Anuradha. Those housed there have been kidnapped or tricked into sexual slavery, and many will have been given severe sexually transmitted infections, including HIV. Despite stories of absolute horror and abuse, Anuradha and her small team have built a haven at Maiti Nepal for about 700 women and girls. The scale and intensity of the suffering these females have endured is almost beyond comprehension, as is the depth of commitment and inspiration that Anuradha and her team have brought to bear in their attempts to help. The devastating news is that, according to no less an authority than Anuradha herself, the good work of Maiti Nepal is only able to help a fraction of the thousands and thousands that are suffering.

So on that final afternoon in Nepal, Joanna and our team set off to visit Maiti. The sunshine was glorious. On arrival we were met by a multitude of beaming faces. Literally hundreds of young children dressed in every bright colour you can imagine. I was startled by the power of their joy. It was almost bemusing in the light of what we learned later that day about just how much these young, and some very young, girls had suffered. How can such vulnerable people endure so much and still express so much happiness?

As had happened a dozen times during the trip, we were garlanded as we made our way down the long line assembled to greet us. Over the next couple of hours, we watched a series of plays and dances all put together and performed by the residents. Then Anuradha asked Joanna if she would become a global ambassador for Maiti Nepal. I don't really think there was any way that Joanna could say no. Nonetheless, she graciously accepted the honour.

Our final evening in Nepal was marked by a great gathering of the team and the media entourage. The Dwarika hotel had a huge open courtyard, all around which were ornate flowerbeds and beautiful trees. One area was set out with tables and we agreed that we should have dinner outside that evening, and a few drinks. What a group we made. All the different people thrust together in the mad adventure that was the Nepal trip. Joanna's son Jamie did a pretty impressive Elvis impersonation, complete with gyrating hips and turned-up collar. The lawyers sang their hearts out. David Howe was something akin to a human jukebox – he knew, and could sing and play, an amazing amount of tunes. Typical of this trip, even our celebration 'do' couldn't pass without incident. Imagine the happy scene – our great group of forty-odd happy, singing, celebrating Gurkha Justice team members basking in the warmth of a humid evening in this lovely hotel. Then suddenly, an extremely irate man descended upon the scene. He was highly agitated, veins bulging in his temples. His arms were gesticulating wildly and he was shouting with such force that it was making him strain and stand on his tiptoes. I was convinced that he had a German accent and I was not the only one – I heard muttered references to bathing towels and sun loungers and, quite reprehensibly, someone hummed a few bars of the *Dam Busters* theme. It appeared that the man was incandescent with rage because we were singing and being happy. By now I was trying to find Jeremy Beadle or, possibly, Basil Fawlty – this could not be serious. The man ranted and raved, principally to David Howe who had committed the cardinal sin of being the one holding the guitar. David adopted that open-mouthed, arms outstretched posture that people do when trying to appease 'Mr Angry'. So there we were, Joanna Lumley's lot, being harangued for getting rowdy.

To our slight embarrassment, we later found out that he wasn't actually German. I think he was Swiss. Alastair Leithhead of the BBC thought we were all being 'wussy' and I was to find out that he had gone and had a 'bit of a word'. Still, there's usually a bit of row at any decent party.

And so the whole mad chaotic adventure of the trip was over. Only the long flight home was left. And we returned home drained, exhausted and exhilarated all at the same time.

REFLECTIONS ON A JOURNEY

I had never been involved in a campaign as big as this. I'd never been to Nepal. I had never experienced the rush of emotion that comes from looking at the people you have been trying so long to help once they have actually got what they wanted, and what they deserved. I had never organised anything like this trip. The Gurkha Justice campaign was overflowing with firsts. Looking back, letting the images and the conversations flood back into my mind, it feels like watching a film with someone else in it.

As I've got older, I've suddenly become aware just how much life is like a labyrinth of connections. You can trace many of the big things that happen back to small instances in the past, which in turn lead to other, larger events, which then grow into something more, until we end up where we are today. Out of tiny moments, passing conversations and brief meetings, which at the time seem almost inconsequential, huge things develop.

So it was for Sharon Hendy. Sharon is living proof of my belief that small beginnings can lead to dramatic endings. In her capacity as a feature writer for *The Sun*, Sharon came with us on our visit to Nepal. For her, the trip was to lead to a meeting with someone who moved her so deeply that she has researched, written and had published a book inspired by their story. It looks very much as though the book will now be made into a major Hollywood film. It even reached the White House and Sharon received a personal letter from Hillary Clinton congratulating her on her work. All of this came about as a direct result of her decision to come to Nepal with us. But how did it happen?

The Sun had reported on Prince Charles's donation of the proceeds from the sale of one of his paintings, which helped to purchase the land Maiti Nepal was built on, and they had gone on to support the charity themselves and raise funds for an extension.

On the last day of our tour, when we all went to visit the charity, by the time Sharon arrived the rest of us were already on a tour of the building. Sharon asked Anuradha if there was someone she could speak with who would encapsulate the mission of Maiti and there, walking across the garden, came Radhika with her young son. Radhika and Sharon were to talk for many hours. Radhika poured out a story of terrible suffering and abuse, of separation from her son and of her desperate flight to freedom. Out of this conversation came the book, Radhika's Story.

Sharon's retelling of Radhika's plight will play a major role in exposing the dire world of trafficking and abuse. By that means, it will help many people. The money raised from the sale of the book will go a long way towards transforming Radhika's life. The film will do even more to help raise the profile of this issue. And in an odd way, all of this can be traced back to four retired Gurkhas knocking on a door in Folkestone.

SEVENTEEN

DRIPPING TOXIN

❧

J oanna and the campaign were to win a long and impressive list of awards and plaudits. Howe & Co. also received much recognition and prestige as a result of their work for the cause.

Due to her busy schedule, Joanna was unable to accept some of her prizes in person and I often collected them on her behalf. She won Communicator of the Year at the PRWeek Awards in the autumn of 2009 but couldn't go, so Lynne and I went in her place.

In terms of PR and campaigning, these are the most prestigious of all the industry awards and, though I do not usually confess to being impressed by the lavish-ness of these events, they are quite imposing, with over 1,200 guests. As Communicator of the Year was one of the major awards of the evening, the recipient, or in this case, the person standing in for the recipient, was expected to say a few words. This, I dutifully did, but there was an almost audible feeling of disappointment that it was I, and not Joanna, who would be accepting the gong. That said, the campaign itself received a rousing reception. This meant all the more to me coming from the professionals of the communication and campaigning world.

There was to be an amusing campaign-based diversion concerning the table for Virgin Atlantic. The direct-action group Plane Stupid, which usually campaigns against aviation using pretty up-front tactics, had, on this occasion, been unusually subtle. They are renowned for climbing up buildings and chaining themselves to fences in order to try and make their point. However, that evening they arrived in evening wear, blended in completely and took all the seats at the Virgin Atlantic table. Eventually, the police arrived, much to the horror and stress of Danny Rogers, editor of PRWeek and host for the evening.

On another occasion, we were all invited to the *Daily Mirror* Pride of Britain Awards at the Grosvenor House Hotel, Park Lane. Joanna had been voted by the *Mail*'s readers as Public Figure of the Year for her work on behalf of the Gurkhas. Lynne and I travelled to the venue in Joanna and Stephen's car. We swept up the approach road to the main ballroom entrance and stepped out onto the red carpet. Of course, Joanna was the only person of interest in our party to the phalanx of press photographers.

It was a lovely evening. The room was wall to wall with celebrities. As I walked to the loo I passed Michael Caine, Gordon Brown, Louis Walsh and Simon Cowell, all in just one trip.

Later in the evening, during that milling about period after the main event and before everyone goes home, I stood next to someone who I thought looked vaguely recognisable. When I asked someone in that 'don't look behind you but who's that over there' way who the familiar face was, they told me it was Frank Lampard. Only minutes later, as I walked with Lynne and Joanna to find the door that would take them to the smoking area, we passed a blonde lady who said a very cheery 'hello'. 'Who's that?' I asked Joanna. Even Joanna thought my ignorance a little amusing and laughingly replied, 'Peter dear, that's Baby Spice.' How would I know?

As well as the award ceremonies, there were a number of truly lovely follow-up events and visits. Joanna kindly agreed to open the Christmas Fair at Guston Primary School, just outside Dover. Guston is the local school for many of the Gurkha children whose fathers are based at Connaught Barracks. She made a reasonably lengthy road trip down from London to open this small event. To the school, the parents and the pupils it meant a very great deal indeed. Celebrities so often get bad press for their lifestyle or perceived poor behaviour. From what

I gather, it was typical of Joanna that she would so willingly invest so much time making an appearance such as the one at Guston, completely out of the eye of the media.

Then, there was a trip to Folkestone to witness and share in the Gurkhas receiving the freedom of the town. We combined this visit with a 'round Kent Gurkha tour'. We started at the Freedom of Folkestone, where the currently serving Gurkhas exercised their newly given right to march through Folkestone with 'bayonets drawn and bands playing'. Then we moved on to visit the Oddfellows Hall in Broomfield Road, Cheriton (also in Folkestone), which had become the social hub for so many veterans. Next, we called in at the gleaming new Folkestone Academy. Well before any involvement with Gurkha Justice, Joanna had been invited to choose a colour for one of the school's four houses, and that 'yellow' house was named 'Lumley House' in her honour. After that, it was off to Cranbrook to meet the lady who had touched my arm that day whilst I was petitioning and thus played a tiny, but crucial, part in the drama of our campaign.

Once the campaign had reached its successful conclusion, I had decided to try and find the woman responsible for Joanna's involvement in our fight. She was just one of many who had signed the petition that Saturday in Cranbrook, so she'd be hard to track down, and I couldn't even work my way through the list of names on the petition since I'd handed it in to Downing Street.

I contacted my local newspaper, the *Kent Messenger*, which covers most of Kent in a variety of local editions. They ran a story in the Weald edition saying I was seeking 'The Mystery Woman', quite a risky headline for a would-be MP, and eventually we located one Annie Watsham – she was thrilled to have been remembered. So it came about that our last engagement on that day was to take Joanna to Cranbrook to meet Annie.

By now, I was good friends with Howard Cox who lived in Cranbrook. He was and remains very involved in all things to do with the local community in and around Cranbrook. He had helped spread the word of our visit and called on the mobile during our trip from Folkestone to Cranbrook to report that there were at least a couple of hundred 'Cranbookians' waiting to greet Joanna.

My great friend Joe Underwood had acted as driver for our day. Joe finally got us to Cranbrook, slightly late due to the obligatory tractor on the road. Joanna opened the car door to a great roar of approval from the crowd. Joanna and Annie met on the exact spot outside the Vestry Hall where we had stood all those months before gathering signatures.

I reflected on my long-held view that sometimes it's the smallest things that we say or do that can have the biggest consequences. What if Annie hadn't been there that day? What if she hadn't suggested Joanna? What if she had and I hadn't acted on her suggestion?

Usually, time spent with Joanna was always compromised by the need to keep to a tight schedule, or to deal with a pressing media crowd or to plot what needed to be done next. There was, at the end of that long fun-packed day, a wonderful hour spent in the back garden of Annie's beautiful Cranbrook cottage eating straw-berries. This was a lovely moment of closure on the 'Cranbrook link'.

Inevitably, the furore of the campaign faded. The frequency of contact between the Holy Trinity of Joanna, the lawyers and I reduced as the necessities of our normal lives slowly drew us all back down to earth.

The campaign victory had been greeted with joy and relief in pretty much all corners of the UK. Many people commented that it had actually made the 'coun-try feel good about itself'. However, as ever in life, events were to prove that you can't please everyone.

As our fight had continued over the years, and particularly in the intense six-month period after Joanna became involved, I had experienced a grow-ing realisation that the upper echelons of the MoD and the government were the main force of opposi-tion to our campaign. The overwhelming majority of serving members of the Armed Forces, many of whom had worked with the Gurkhas, were in favour of our mission. However, deep in the recesses of the MoD, the true enemy lay.

So it was not a surprise when, nearly a whole year after our victory, the vested interest that had so might-ily resented our victory once again found a vehicle for its expression and was to briefly reunite the Gurkha Justice campaign.

The Home Affairs Select Committee that had played such a key role in the run-up to our victory under the chairmanship of Keith Vaz MP (he of the apple peeling) continued to discuss Gurkha matters. This was entirely within its normal remit.

The intense inter-faction conflict between the many and various groups that represent retired Gurkhas had led to a huge degree of mistrust between them. For a considerable period of time, there had been rumours and allegations that one group of Gurkhas was 'ripping off' another group of Gurkhas. One particular piece of hearsay related to access to legal advice back in Nepal. One of the great unsung heroes of the Gurkha Justice campaign was the Legal Services Commission. They had made the decision that retired Gurkhas should have access to legal aid – without that, the whole vital legal strand of the campaign would have been seriously hampered. Now there were rumours that groups of unscrupulous retired Gurkhas (or people acting on their behalf) were pressuring individuals to pay a sum of money (said to be about £500) for access to British lawyers. As these lawyers were already in receipt of legal aid, any such arrangement would have been, literally, criminal. When these rumours first surfaced, Howe & Co. reported them to the British government suggesting that these should be investigated.

At the Home Affairs Select Committee of 9 March 2010, Kevan Jones MP, a junior Defence Minister whose antagonism we had previously encountered, commented on these 'rogue solicitors', as they were being termed. Howe & Co. took the view that the comments he made were an implied slur on their reputation. Not only that, Jones had said that many retired Gurkhas were coming to Britain with no proper knowledge of what they were, and were not, entitled to, that Joanna had been silent on this issue and that this 'irritated' him. He implied that Joanna (and by definition I) should have kept fighting and campaigning for the Gurkhas.

Mr Jones's comments gave the impression that Joanna had been 'parachuted' into the issue, had taken the plaudits and had then abandoned the retired Gurkhas. Nothing could be further from the truth and it completely missed the point that she was a 'daughter of the regiment' who lived and breathed the cause. It ignored the fact that she had consistently undertaken many acts of kindness, completely out of the eye of the media, to help the retired Gurkhas. She had, on occasion, been so upset by the difficulties that individual Gurkha families were facing while the likes of Mr Jones were busy opposing us, that she had given me money to pass on to various groups of Gurkhas in order to relieve their poverty.

This had to be challenged. The implication that Joanna had 'let down' retired Gurkhas was totally unfounded. The idea that Howe & Co. were in any way associated with improper conduct relating to legal aid was quite frankly defamatory and had to be addressed.

Joanna was thoroughly used to the way issues could be played one way then another in the media.

She knew that they could 'turn on a sixpence' and that sometimes it was entirely the right thing to do to effectively say 'No comment' and let the story dissipate by itself. However, lines had been crossed. Not only were these comments unpleasant and factually untrue, threatening the reputations of those of us in the 'eye' of the campaign, myself included, they were now threatening something even more important – the good faith and trust that hundreds of thousands of people had invested in us, in our cause and in the retired Gurkhas. We were on the cusp of that whole ocean of good feeling that a great wrong had been put right turning into a sour belief that nothing had been what it seemed. I was furious. Sue Reid of the *Daily Mail* had written some stories highlighting the circumstances that some retired Gurkhas had found themselves in on arrival in Britain – 'Living in poverty and convinced they were exploited...' The issue was now spreading into the national media.

For decade after decade we as a country had subjected our 'never more faithful friends' the Gurkhas to unbelievable injustices: appalling pensions, dreadful terms of service, poor pay and the refusal of settlement rights in the country they were prepared to fight and possibly die for. Against this background, a small team of people had taken on the entire might of the British government and won. We had won in every battle we had undertaken, including in the court of public opinion. This had all been done with the purest of motives, with next to no money but with an abundance of passion, energy and downright doggedness. The swell of public support had been truly remarkable. The British public had spoken out and we had won against incredible odds. Now we were facing the dripping toxin of allegations and smears designed to sour and undermine.

I said to Joanna that I believed we had to come out fighting on this, not to defend our reputations, but to reassure all those countless thousands of supporters that they had backed a truly just cause and a campaign of integrity.

We conferred. I spoke with the Number 10 press office asking if they could clarify who, or which government department, was behind these comments. Was Mr Jones speaking as an individual expressing a personal opinion? Was he reflecting an official government point of view? Did the Prime Minister, Gordon Brown, share his view?

In the end, we resolved to call a press conference. And what better place than the Atrium restaurant at Millbank Studios just opposite the Houses of Parliament, the venue which we had used for that pivotal press conference with Phil Woolas MP about a year before.

On the day of the press conference, Joanna was anxious. Lynne and I went to her home to prepare. I felt for Joanna. Her role in the campaign had been brilliant. She had handled every situation with almost perfect poise. She had done it all with the utmost goodwill. Yet the murky world of politics was now threatening the entire aura of the campaign and everything for which she had worked so hard. We talked it through a couple of times. We were doing this to reassure all the campaign's supporters. She reiterated her concern that the media could turn savagely. I reiterated mine – that sometimes you have to take things head on.

Word of our plans had now reached Downing Street and the press office called to intervene. Would Joanna speak with the Prime Minister to clear up any 'misunderstanding'? Once again, this was to be a major judgment call on how to handle an issue. To have encouraged Joanna to take this call would probably have secured the Prime Minister's support and a public comment from him that Mr Jones was 'out of order'. However, this would not have achieved as high a profile in the media as had the original offensive remarks. I told Downing Street that Joanna was 'unavailable'. She remained 'unavailable' to Downing Street on a number of occasions in the next few hours.

Press interest was surprisingly intense. Penny Marshall of ITN called. She asked if she and her crew might ride with Joanna and me in our cab for the journey to the press conference. I explained that we would want those important few minutes to prepare for the event in private. She was wonderfully persuasive, listing the merits of me changing my view, but I was equally firm in holding my ground.

This was one of the few occasions where I felt that my presence was of help to Joanna. We journeyed together to Millbank. When we arrived, the room was already packed. The microphones and cameras were ready and we were off.

We had planned how to start. We would lead by saying that we had convened the press conference to publicly ask the Prime Minister to reaffirm the government's faith in their decision to allow Gurkhas to live in the UK and also to reassure the public that they had backed a right and just cause.

We refuted the allegations against us with passion. In fact, later, on *Sky News*, defence correspondent Geoff Meade was to say that he couldn't recall a press conference where emotions had run so high. One journalist asked if we had 'fought the wrong campaign' and suggested that we should have tackled the pensions issue before fighting for settlement rights. I responded that we (or, at the time it all started in 2004, I) had not gone looking for this campaign and that it had only started because the retired Gurkhas themselves had wanted it to. Martin Howe reinforced the point, stating that we had won a choice for the retired Gurkhas – there was no compulsion for them to leave Nepal, but they could now enjoy the same rights as the soldiers from other Commonwealth countries. That is, after four years' service they could settle in Britain if they so wished.

Others pressed the point about 'middlemen' charging retired Gurkhas back in Nepal for access to British lawyers who were being paid for by legal aid. We all concurred that if that was happening, then it was totally wrong, and that it should be thoroughly investigated and anyone involved should be punished. Martin Howe used this opportunity to point out that, in fact, the British government were one of the chief 'money makers' out of Gurkha visas – retired Gurkhas had to pay over £700 for a visa to settle in the UK at that time. This was a huge sum of money to the average retired Gurkha, and the situation was made much worse by the fact that this fee needed to be paid for each family member. Surely this must be wrong, Martin declared, as the retired Gurkhas being forced to pay these fees now had a legal right to settle here.

David Enright made an impassioned contribution in which he set out some of the financial contributions that Joanna had personally made to help individual Gurkha families and Martin explained that, since Mr Jones had implied that Howe & Co. might be one of those very 'rogue' legal advisers, the firm had been subject to an almost Stasi-like investigation and review of its activities by the government body responsible for ensuring compliance with the terms of legal aid. Martin took great pleasure in being able to reveal that the report from the investigating body had now been released and had completely exonerated Howe & Co. of any wrongdoing.

At around the same time as our press conference was beginning Mr Jones issued a full apology. About an hour later, I received yet another call from Downing Street asking again if the Prime Minister might speak with Joanna. She took the call on my mobile in the staircase hallway of the Millbank building. He too apologised.

After the call, Joanna gave each of us a little memento of our campaigning time together. It was a miniature Gurkha hat with a slot down the centre of the hat top to hold a place name or card. We left and made our separate ways home.

Text of Mr Jones's apology:

I apologise unreservedly for any offence caused to Joanna Lumley by my remarks to the Home Affairs Committee – this was not intended.

I have the greatest of respect for Joanna for the superb work that she has done on Gurkha issues. And I know that the whole nation has immense respect for the bravery and courage shown by the Gurkhas now and in the past.

I want to put on the record that I accept that Joanna and her campaign did not seek to mislead Gurkhas about the life that they could expect if they relocated to the UK.

My sole concern, and that of this government, with which I know Joanna agrees, is to stop unscrupulous middlemen ripping off and misleading vulnerable ex-Gurkhas who are entitled to settle in the UK when our free service already exists to help them without charge.

EIGHTEEN

AND STILL IT DRIPS

———————◆———————

The apology of Mr Jones, reinforced as it was by the apology of Mr Brown, resolved matters. Or so we thought. Another year passed – then, in the early part of 2011, the MP for Aldershot, Gerald Howarth, entered the arena on the topic of Gurkha settlement.

Mr Howarth made some comments to various media outlets, voicing his concerns that local services in and around Aldershot were in danger of being 'overwhelmed' by the influx of retired Gurkha soldiers and their families. The fact that Mr Howarth is a properly elected Member of Parliament gives him a legitimate platform to express his views about his local community. The fact that he is a junior minister in the Ministry of Defence strengthens this platform.

I had been asked by Radio Surrey to take part in one of their news programmes. The Puffins had become the temporary home of Lynne's daughter and our three lively three- and four-year-old grandchildren. They needed somewhere to stay, having left one house and now experiencing some problems securing their new property. The interview was to be by telephone and I decided to take the call in the small attic room above the kitchen end of the house. Here, I could avoid interjections from Jack, aged four, asking if he could play 'Angry Birds' on my iPad, whilst trying to answer some particularly tricky point posed by a pressing interviewer – even though I've done a lot of radio appearances, questions about 'Angry Birds' can still throw me!

The interview began. As is the custom, the interviewer played a package of comments relevant to the issue before starting the questions. Mr Howarth MP advocated that the retired Gurkhas should be 'dispersed', as had been the case with asylum seekers. A degree of cold fury formed in my mind. Was this an MP pandering to a part of his local community who resented outsiders? Or, even more unpleasant, was this how he genuinely understood the issue? Was this what he felt? How would the retired Gurkhas now living in his area feel – many of them full British citizens? Here was an MP advocating that some British citizens shouldn't live in certain parts of Britain. I would have thought that anyone with any understanding of an MP's role would be able to see how offensive these views were. But no, Mr Howarth seemed settled in his opinion.

And it was to get worse. There was the direct implication that, somehow, it was my and Joanna's responsibility to make sure that the various levels of government had come together to provide any extra services for the Gurkhas. Groups had appeared on Facebook and Twitter on which local residents were venting their anger and frustration towards the Gurkhas. One was called 'Joanna Lumley F**ked Up our Town'. Another was called 'Lumley's Legacy'.

I just couldn't let this go. Within minutes of the interview's end I was drafting letters to the Prime Minister and to Nick Clegg. I found these easy to write, fuelled as they were with a sense of anger.

Over the next few weeks there were to be a whole series of similar interviews. I had to counter one caller to James Whale's *Drivetime* show on LBC who said, 'It's OK for you, I doubt you live in Aldershot.' The clear implication being that I obviously didn't and must instead live in some part of the country where Gurkhas weren't a feature – or, rather, a problem. For good measure, the caller chipped in that 'they [the Gurkhas] bring all their relatives and family you know, some of them thirty-five each'! By now I was pacing around the office, trying to burn up the energy generated by my sense of frustration. I reminded the caller calmly (honestly!) that whilst I didn't live in Aldershot, I did live in Folkestone, currently the home town of serving Gurkhas. As a result, I was surrounded by the many retired Gurkhas who had chosen to make east Kent their home after leaving the army. I ate in Gurkha restaurants, shopped in Gurkha shops and was often picked up from the station by Gurkha taxis.

As for the 'thirty-five relatives', I relayed the story of the three children of a retired Gurkha who had been denied access to Britain in the most distressing of circumstances. I first met their mother in the William Harvey hospital, Ashford. She was dying of inoperable cancer. She had already overcome great tragedy in her life: her Gurkha husband had been banned from living in Britain after his retirement, dying some years before our campaign and the resultant change in the rules. Now here was Anuka, desperately ill; her family back in Nepal. She had come to Britain to forge a better life and was trying to 'regularise' her status before bringing over her children. When her diagnosis was confirmed, however, her three children couldn't even get a visa to enter Britain to see her during her final days. With advice from Howe & Co., a letter from Joanna and a stream of emails from me, they fought the system and won through. The three children did get to see their dying mother. But the fact that we had to fight so hard to get them into the country, even in these most extreme circumstances, shows just how tight and restrictive the rules are. The right of settlement extends, in all but exceptional cases, to the retired Gurkha, his wife and dependent children. 'Dependent' is usually defined as under eighteen. The idea that a retired Gurkha can bring thirty-five dependents to Britain is laughable. The fact that such nonsense gains traction in local communities shows just how important it is for everyone involved, particularly those in elected office, to keep facts at the forefront of their argument and avoid pandering to ridiculous extremism.

During this uprising of ill-feeling emanating from the Aldershot & Rushmoor area, I also contacted one of the key players behind the 'Lumley's Legacy' movement. To my surprise, despite the strident and, on occasion, outrageous views expressed on his sites and forums, I found him rather amenable and balanced. I sensed that here was a person I could talk to genuinely and try to encourage to take a different perspective. We spoke at length. He explained that he saw pressure building in Aldershot & Rushmoor; I challenged him on his singling out of Joanna as the one responsible. Over the weeks we kept in touch and I understand that he, and many of his colleagues, are now actively engaged in trying to encourage better integration of the two communities.

Both the Prime Minister and the deputy Prime Minister replied to Joanna's letter and mine. I was struck by the content and tone of David Cameron's response. Faced with an MP speaking out in such strong terms, he could so easily have fudged the issue. He did not. He reaffirmed his government's stance on the Gurkha issue. I felt relieved.

The decision to allow retired Gurkhas who had left the British Army prior to 1997 to settle in the UK was enthusiastically, and in my mind quite properly, taken up by the Conservatives. Indeed, without their help, for which I give them all handsome credit, the campaign may have faltered – it is highly unlikely that we would have won the Opposition Day motion that gave the campaign its decisive political edge without them. My understanding is that Mr Cameron himself actually voted in support of giving retired Gurkhas the right to live in Britain.

As a result of the furore over the situation in Aldershot, Cameron, Clegg and the Secretary of State for Communities and Local Government, Eric Pickles, worked extremely hard to find a sum of money to help with the integration of retired Gurkhas in Aldershot, Rushmoor and elsewhere. Joanna and I were both grateful for and impressed by their commitment. These were not easy days to be finding any government money to do anything at all.

The Prime Minister offered Joanna and me the opportunity to meet Eric Pickles. Despite his reputation as a political bruiser, Pickles positively radiated a desire to do right by the Gurkhas and Joanna and I left reassured that it was the intention of the coalition government to stand behind their commitment to the veterans.

That said, Mr Howarth's views and his attitude towards the retired Gurkhas are so much at odds with those of his Prime Minister and government that I simply do not understand how he can continue in his position as a junior Defence Minister.

I challenge Mr Howarth's views on a number of fronts. Aldershot and the army go together like Davenport and the navy or Lincolnshire and the Royal Air Force. Gurkhas have a long and proud record of serving and living in and around Aldershot and Farnborough – military life and Aldershot life are woven together and have been for decades. It was always going to be the case that retired Gurkhas would settle in the communities that they know.

Mr Howarth implied that the government had made its decision to allow retired Gurkhas to settle in the UK on an 'emotional' basis when confronted by our campaign. What an extraordinary thing to say. Should we construct our society without taking emotion fully into account? What kind of emotion was at work when we were routinely refusing entry to Britain to the likes of Tul Bahadur Pun VC and Lechiman Gurung VC, and Gyanendra Rai who was so severely injured in the Falkland Islands? My interpretation of the Gurkha Justice campaign was that it was quite deliberately and properly emotional. The nation asked itself if it was prepared to see soldiers who had fought for the British Army, some of whom had won the highest awards for bravery, forbidden the right to live here with us. If that's emotional, I plead guilty – as, I imagine, would hundreds of thousands of others.

It seems that part of the language of the debate in Aldershot has turned away from 'retired British Army veterans' to 'Nepalese immigrants'. In my opinion, Mr Howarth's language seems to encourage this. We are in danger of losing sight of the essential fact that the vast majority of retired Gurkhas, even the elderly ones, now living in and around Aldershot are there precisely because they are British Army veterans.

I wonder what the reaction would be if a Scottish regiment had been based in the area for a prolonged period and many people of Scottish descent had settled there. Would there still be a call for them to be shared out? How much of the 'grave concern' that some now refer to is because the Gurkhas and their families look different?

Interestingly, on his website Mr Howarth says: 'I represent everyone in Aldershot – not just those who voted for me.' This seems to me to be at odds with his view that retired British Army Gurkhas should be encouraged to go to other parts of the country.

For many years migration to the UK has been running at levels of around 200,000 per annum. On the second anniversary of the Gurkha Justice campaign victory, the Home Office revealed figures that showed the total number of retired Gurkhas and their family members who had applied for a visa was running at about 4,000. Compared to the vast numbers associated with migration patterns into and out of Britain, this is a truly tiny number.

NINETEEN

JOANNA, DAUGHTER OF NEPAL AND GODDESS OF THE GURKHAS

———————•———————

When teams of people are suddenly thrust together in the pursuit of a great dream or quest I think the relationships that are formed can be likened to the reactions that take place when atoms get smashed together in a nuclear reactor. The people or particles are hurled together, make and release a lot of energy, then the team or atomic structure disintegrates and each particle whizzes off in its own direction. The Gurkha Justice campaign was no different. In its later stages it was incredibly demanding and pressured. The political and media world in which we were working changed incredibly quickly and we had to think on our feet and adapt to events at great speed. The interest from people and the world became intense. We were often incredibly tired as we all, including Joanna, had day jobs. Added to this was the enormous emotional bond that we felt with the Gurkha community. In a normal working environment, challenges can be looked on as merely professional tasks, although there may be a great sense of pride in working hard and skilfully to sort out a problem or achieve some progress. But for us, the Gurkha campaign was different. We had looked these men in the eye and seen and felt their hurt and anger. We had been humbled by the stories we had heard of what they had endured. We had actually met and talked with living Gurkha legends. This issue didn't so much get under our skin as get into our soul. The need to just keep going bordered on the irrational. I suspect that any consideration of the odds of success in the early years of 2004 to 2007 would have persuaded most people that this venture, worthy though it was, was going to achieve little more than raising the issue's profile.

So many events, large and small, so many factors, predicted and unpredicted, and so many people combined to make the campaign a success. The amalgamation of the legal, political and public threads was crucial. And it wouldn't have succeeded without a large dose of absolute determination. On several occasions, we also had that all-important element of luck. That is why every single person who did anything – be it sign a petition or write to their MP – should feel an immense sense of pride in their contribution. It could be said that those of us in the 'eye of the storm' were fortunate to be able to play a larger part in solving an issue in which we passionately believed. To single out any one individual would almost detract from the contribution of others. However, this was a campaign that was to propel one person, Joanna Lumley, into the hearts and minds of two nations in a way that demands some comment and special recognition.

We live in an age in which 'celebrity' matters. To most of those that study the body politic and how we live as a community, the role of celebrities is fascinating. To others, it's almost objectionable. The media follow celebrity for the simple reason that they know the vast majority of people are interested in them and what they do. How often have you 'tutted' in your mind about how ridiculous it is that every nuance and detail of a certain person's life is the subject of acres of media coverage – only to find you reading it yourself?

The world is full of enormous suffering. We all know that. Just as an example, think of the horrendous daily torment and death in just one place: Africa. Yet, the undeniable truth is that so many of us know about these terrible situations, but don't actually do anything about it unless prompted. It is a proven fact that if a celebrity goes and visits a warzone or the scene of a famine and receives media attention, many more of us will take notice and give money or time to help. This used to upset me. Now I accept it as just the way we are. We can know that something should be done, but not do it until we are led to do so. A more generous interpretation of this might be that we all live busy lives that are so crowded with thoughts and actions that our self-defence mechanism is simply for those other bigger issues to get crowded out.

There are also issues, like the Gurkhas, that most people simply don't know about. We had a group of politicians in Westminster who were not minded to give the campaign the benefit of 'high priority' treatment, despite knowing very well that the Gurkhas were fine warriors and that they were badly treated in comparison with other Commonwealth soldiers. But among the population at large, I genuinely think that most did not realise the injustices that were part of the Gurkha history and current situation. Some older people who might have had first- or second-hand experience relating to the Second World War seemed to understand the enormous contribution that successive generations had given our country. They knew of the Gurkha record of courage and service. But even they seemed unaware of the reasons behind our campaign. And so we were fighting for an issue that the public as a whole knew little or nothing about.

So many causes, charities and commercial companies use celebrity endorsement as a means of raising their profile or their sales. On many occasions, the link between the product or cause and the celebrity seems absurd. George Foreman and his lean mean grilling machine spring to mind. What on earth does Mr Foreman know about grilling? Why should a man capable of pulverising your brains be able to influence which grilling machine you buy? I also question situations in which a celebrity is used in a superficial way to try and advance a cause. If the celebrity has no insight or empathy with the matter in hand, this can so easily look insincere. I remember in the 1980s when British Leyland tried to 'sex up' the worthy (but definitely un-sporty) Mini Metro by sticking an MG badge on it. Did that really ever persuade someone that they were buying something with a 'sports' heritage?

It is hard to think that there could have been any other person so perfectly positioned by virtue of personality, image, family background and intelligence to lead our campaign as Joanna. She was extremely well known. Most people liked her. Her fame and popularity had not come as a result of riotous and dubious partying and behaviour. She appealed to a wide range of ages. And most powerfully, when it came to engaging with the military and politicians, she was 'a daughter of the regiment'. Her family were part of the issue. She encapsulated a certain Britishness, to the point of almost being a national treasure. She had the ability to handle herself exquisitely in all situations. Quite simply, her involvement in the Gurkha Justice campaign was a mixture of the 'absolutely fabulous' and the 'absolutely crucial'.

I was to work with Joanna at close quarters for some

nine months. Joanna, Lynne and I experienced some exhilarating highs and some heartbreaking lows. Despite the fact that we did not know each other before my first telephone conversation with her in early September 2008, we were to exchange barely a cross word for the duration of our time together, even when coping with situations that were unprecedented in any of our lives.

Looking back, perhaps part of the smoothness of our working relationship could be linked to my view of celebrity: I simply don't understand our fascination with it. I was to prove this by showing that I couldn't identify certain celebrities even if they passed me in the street (or, as was to happen, in the hotel ballroom). And even if I did recognise them, I just couldn't find it within myself to treat them any differently from any other person. This included Joanna. I always tried to treat Joanna as the highly intelligent, committed person she is – rather than as a 'celeb'.

Many months after the campaign, when Joanna, the lawyers and I had to swing back into action to refute the particularly unpleasant comments made by Kevan Jones about the campaign, Joanna was asked by a journalist, 'Is it right for celebrities to get involved in politics?' Joanna cut him to shreds with her curtly delivered response: 'I'm not a celebrity, I'm an actress.' Quite a line. Maybe the fact that she didn't consider herself to be a celebrity at all was another reason why we got on so well.

I felt a sense of responsibility for Joanna with

regard to her role in the campaign. I had made that first fateful call which resulted in her involvement. Even though she learned the detail incredibly quickly I felt it was my role to make sure that she was always fully briefed. Martin, David and Kieran played a part in this too. They would give Joanna all the background she needed so that she would be fully prepared for any interview that related to a legal matter. The press conferences could be very demanding. We would often have dozens of photographers and media crews in attendance and each would have their own demands for a live or pre-recorded interview. Sometimes, I had Sky pleading to have Joanna 'live' for the top of one of their bulletins, and the BBC arguing the same. The press people would all want their bite of the cherry too. All these running conflicts had to be managed with Joanna left as untroubled as possible and all the various media crews feeling that they had been given their fair share of access. Managing this was almost a job in its own right, and at various times I was referred to as her PA, her media manager, her bodyguard and, on one hilarious occasion, her husband.

The only time I feared for Joanna's physical safety was in those first few minutes as we emerged in the arrivals hall at Kathmandu airport on our visit to Nepal. The crush was overwhelming and intimidating. It took us all by surprise. There was no aggression or intent to harm – there were just so many people there that they naturally presented a serious threat to safety.

I was never appointed as the person to take the lead in such circumstances. Like so many things in the campaign, it just happened that way.

Joanna and I exchanged emails day in day out, usually late into the night, as did the lawyers and the other members of our campaign team. In addition to these emails and between ourselves, Lynne and I started to receive letters and cards addressed to our home (which was effectively the campaign HQ) for Joanna. These came from people all over the country, praising her and urging her on. We always tried to collate these and forward them on. Most of the letters conveyed the most sincere sentiments and often contained the retelling of family stories relating to Gurkha heroism and devotion. Some were lighter. I recall one MP's letter – a response to one of the many messages that Joanna sent to all MPs – which started: 'My knees trembled on opening your letter when I realised that it was from you...' He later added, by way of an aside, that he supported the campaign. On one occasion, the postman said, slightly nervously, ''Ere mate. I hope you don't mind me asking ... but does she live here with you?'

Letters played a crucial role in this campaign. There were our campaign letters to MPs, some signed by me, others signed by Joanna. There were the hundreds of letters sent in to us by our supporters; the thousands of letters sent to MPs by our supporters. And then there were the letters from Joanna to Gordon Brown. These were crucial in ramping up the pressure that was to eventually get us face-to-face meetings with the Prime Minister.

Although there were a number of such letters, three in particular spring to mind. The first, Joanna penned in her own hand using, as she described it, 'proper handwriting'. We mused on how best to try and ensure that this actually got through to the Prime Minister and resolved on the following plan of action. Joanna was to meet Martin Salter MP, then chair of the Commons All-Party Working Group on Gurkha Affairs. After the event, Joanna described to me a scene that could quite easily have come from a John Le Carré novel. She waited stealthily by a particular lamppost near Parliament and passed the letter by hand to Martin when he arrived. He assured her that this letter would find its way into the Prime Minister's 'red box', which he would take with him to Chequers. Rather surreally, Joanna was spotted by the Met Police Bomb Squad who, when they realised who she was, took her for a spin in a bomb-proof Land Rover.

We resorted to yet more subterfuge on another occasion to try and increase the likelihood that our messages would reach their target. Joanna wrote a further letter, this time taking it to the gates of Downing Street herself. The police officer on the gate – there to keep the likes of al-Qaeda out – was a little flummoxed by being approached by no less a person than Joanna Lumley. The officer explained that it was against procedures for him to take a letter into the house. As I had imagined, he was no match for Joanna, who helped him to overcome his concern and saw that the letter was duly handed across.

The final letter, I drafted. This was to be the only time that Joanna and I had a 'jarring' few words. I had suggested that we needed to do another letter and when Joanna responded there was an unusual tone of frustration in her voice. Her view was that we'd written before and we were just being ignored so why would another letter make any difference. I was at work in Maidstone coping with some pretty frightening commercial times. And Joanna Lumley had snapped at me. Losing my temper, I snapped back – just because the first letters hadn't worked didn't mean we shouldn't be writing any more. I restated our firm belief that letters from Joanna Lumley would have more impact than anything from me or the lawyers. She retorted that she wasn't sure who this 'cipher' Joanna Lumley was any more. If she wasn't sure, I came back, then I damn well wasn't – the briefest moment of discord in an otherwise smooth working relationship. Our normal working harmony was steered back on course by her gracious acknowledgement that I probably didn't need her to take out her stress on me right now – I have to confess that during that period she was right. We resolved that I should draft the letter and she would send it.

I somehow developed the knack of drafting letters and notes for Joanna that mimicked very closely her own style. She wrote letters with a particular use of vocabulary and phrasing which I always felt was a form of painting with words. She was never harsh or aggressive, always gentle and coaxing. Her style gave the impression that she was reluctant to trouble the reader, and there was always a strong statement of the appreciation she would feel if the reader was able even to read the letter, never mind act on it. She never neglected to pay handsome tribute to how busy the reader must be. Reading the letter, even for the most hard-bitten, must have been like hearing soft and beguiling words whispered in an ear. Kieran's reaction to this second letter gave me a little feeling of hidden pleasure. I had set out the Gurkha settlement issue as succinctly as possible, then how we felt the popular mood was reacting to it, pointing out, in particular, that public support was building to a level that meant no reasonable government could ignore it. Kieran was mightily impressed with this letter, reporting back to me that 'only Joanna could have expressed it so well'. To this day, Kieran doesn't know who actually wrote those words.

Much of the detailed work and drafting of correspondence was done by Lynne, the lawyers and me. This was not to say that Joanna wouldn't have taken on this task herself, it just reflected the reality that whilst we were all busy, she was perhaps the busiest. Joanna's interest and commitment in the campaign were total. She was even to phone whilst filming for some project in deepest Africa to check on our progress. And there were moments when she alone was uniquely placed to make a significant contribution.

Joanna was to demonstrate her 'mastery of the moment' skills on a number of crucial occasions. The way that Joanna handled the press after her first meeting with Gordon Brown was a classic example. She boxed him in. A person less skilled in their understanding of how the human psyche works would have been tempted to rush out onto College Green full of anger and vitriol. They might have attacked the Prime Minister and his stance. Undoubtedly, this would have felt good and added more petrol to the fire, but it would have missed the point that she saw so easily – that in the end, we had to make this man, the Prime Minister, do what we wanted. To do that, we had to manipulate rather than threaten. This was the innate politician within Joanna in action.

She was, the next day, to perform with similar skill in the now famous live TV encounter with Phil Woolas, the Immigration Minister. During that press conference she had to use anger tempered by an air of teacher-like disappointment – guiding the man, very publicly, towards getting himself into a situation from which there was no real escape other than by submission.

During the campaign, many people would ask: 'What's it like working with Joanna – what's she like in real life?' It was a lot of fun. There were no airs and graces and none of the tantrums that so many celebrities seem to have, if you can believe the reports in the popular press. Instead, there were countless examples of kindness and patience, and some of considerable humour.

Wherever we went, people would stop and stare and approach Joanna for autographs or ask to have their picture taken with her. She never ran out of patience for this. On one occasion, Joanna and I were at Waterloo waiting for a train to Salisbury to go down to meet with the Gurkha Welfare Trust. As we were sitting in one of the little coffee shops in the station, the man sat near to us realised just who was at the next table. He was with his daughter. He asked in that terribly British way: 'I'm sorry to trouble you, but do you mind me asking if I could have your autograph for my daughter.' Joanna agreed. For that man and the other literally hundreds of people who asked, Joanna always seemed to go the extra mile to put them at ease and make their few seconds with her memorable.

There was to be one side-splitting moment of comedy associated with the 'fame' side of things. We were sitting on the edge of our 'battleground', College Green outside Parliament, having a 'chill out'. A group of excited girls came over to Joanna, all giggles and shrieks of laughter. The leader of the pack was holding a camera, gesticulating with her hands about having a photograph taken. Joanna obliged – she walked into the throng, stretched her arms out to gather them all around her and beamed towards the front ... all this to the bemusement of the girl with the camera. In broken English she explained that they wanted Joanna to take the picture, not be in it. They had no idea who she was. There ensued much hilarity, including from Joanna herself. We laughed until our sides hurt. Obviously, *Absolutely Fabulous* wasn't big on Spanish TV.

A large part of why the campaign was to triumph in the end was due to how we, as a team, planned our moves and reacted to events. A huge amount of time and energy went into this, almost to the point where it was like running a military campaign. That said, this was a deeply emotional issue. We couldn't separate ourselves from that. Each of us had our own emotional bond with the campaign. For Joanna, a lot of this related to her family history and to the fact that her father had actually served with the Gurkhas. And not only had he served with them, he had fought with them in one of the most savage conflicts of the Second World War, in the Far East against the Japanese.

Only twice did I ever see this issue nearly over whelm her emotionally. The first was during her reaction to the new guidelines that the Home Office produced in response to their loss at the September 2008 High Court ruling concerning the 1997 cut-off date. The judge had ordered the Home Office to come up with a revised policy and the government appeared to stubbornly almost ignore this instruction from the court. Eventually, after further court action, the government announced a new policy that seemed to be even more restrictive than the one that the High Court judge had struck down. Joanna's anger was plain for all to see.

The second time didn't relate to anger; it just exposed, for a few fleeting seconds, the full depth of her feelings on this matter. It happened during the whirlwind one-week tour of Nepal. We were all gathered in yet another City Hall. It was a vast cinema-style building. The local Gurkhas had put together a programme of singing and dancing to honour Joanna, but there was to be a further surprise. Martin and his team had been liaising with a group of local Gurkhas who wanted to honour Joanna in a different way. Part way through the proceedings, which were, in time-honoured Gurkha fashion, overrunning, Martin took to the stage and helped the Gurkhas announce their special tribute.

Martin explained that the Gurkhas were to rename a local hill as Mattikhan Lumley view. There was something truly special about this. Nepal is one of those countries that still seems to have an almost spiritual bond with the very land that gives it its form. The gift of renaming this special piece of earth, in her, and crucially, her family's honour, really captured the depth of their feeling. I was watching Joanna as the announcement was made. As the words were said, it appeared as if she clutched for her heart. It caught her unawares and she was, just momentarily, shocked. The moment almost made her choke with emotion. This was raw. This captured all that emotional energy that had been bursting to come out for months. She fought to regain herself. Within seconds, though still clearly affected, she was able to speak and to thank the great gathering. When we managed to get back to the car, she asked me if I'd known about that gift of Lumley view. 'Yes', I replied.

Would we have won without Joanna? Almost certainly not. Would we have given up on the cause, most certainly not.

TWENTY

LOOKING BACK

———————•>———————

I t's like remembering a film. I can see so much of the
Gurkha campaign in my mind's eye in full techni-
color detail, but it sometimes feels as if it didn't really
happen. The players at the centre of the storm did
indeed smash together like sub-atomic particles in a
kind of nuclear reaction. But then it was over, and we
were gently but irresistibly dragged back to normal life,
just as the outgoing tide tugs flotsam from the shore.

For me, the grim commercial realities of life running
a medium-sized company in the aftermath of the greatest financial crisis in history beckoned. For Joanna, it
was theatrical and commercial work. Though she was
undoubtedly already much treasured in the national
psyche, many would judge that her profile was raised
even higher as a result of the campaign. My contact with

her continued sporadically as the campaign receded into the rear view mirror of life.

Joanna and the campaign were to win many awards, and if Joanna was not able to attend, she would very kindly offer me the opportunity to go in her place. In addition, Lynne and I would receive a steady stream of correspondence, mostly about Gurkha matters, at our home, which had been sent there for Joanna. When confronted with the difficulty of finding her home address, people sent it through to The Puffins. The frequency of contact diminished. Having got to know her reasonably well, and seen her in some very testing and unusual situations, it feels faintly comic to see her pop up on the TV screen or to hear her voice on a radio advert when in the car.

When great events affect us in pretty much any sphere of our life, we have a deeply ingrained need to talk it over with the others involved. There must be some evolutionary reason why we do this, but I can't quite work out what it is – maybe when we were all hunter gatherers and had either a great hunting result or a really severe catastrophe, we increased the chances of survival by talking through what happened so we could all learn from the experience and hunt better next time. Whatever, as we all lived so far from each other, there was actually very little time in the aftermath of the campaign to sit and to talk and to reflect. In that sense, it has the feel of some unfinished business.

There was only one occasion when I asked Joanna

straight out, 'Given all the things that you've done and been involved in, how did this fit in?' She answered without hesitation, 'Peter, simply the biggest thing I've ever been involved in.'

The Gurkha Justice campaign stands out as an example of British public opinion winning the day. More than that, this was not the type of public opinion following a fad or a trend. This was deeply considered 'public opinion'. It was expressed from every walk of life and from every strata of society: young old, rich and poor. Joanna would often tell me that her busy days of 'normal' life were filled with shouts and cries from scaffolders, cabbies, workmen, city types, shoppers, Rastafarians and, as she whispered in that Home Affairs Select Committee, from at least one Royal. All these cries were of support. People felt that she and the campaign were allowing their view to be heard and to matter. The swell of the campaign had the power to overturn the establishment, to shift a government's position. People loved that feeling.

That some senior politicians and bureaucrats found that hard to live with is understandable, but is slightly souring.

At one of Joanna and my meetings with senior MoD and Home Office staff, I remember how one civil servant drifted off into an unguarded moment and talked of her questioning if she and her colleagues had 'done the right thing' by opposing the move so completely. She had resolved with her inner being that she and they had. I have done the same. On the occasional quiet evening when I sit on the balcony at home that gives me a sumptuous view over a part of the Elham valley, some of the memories flow back to me of all those exciting days. Yes, sometimes I mull over that question – did we do the right thing?

One Saturday evening, I had stood up and was leaning slightly over the balcony wall looking at the beautiful green undulating view. Out of the corner of my eye, I caught the shimmer of a turquoise silk sari, just for a couple of seconds. Leaning forward as I was, I could just see where the end of our steep and crumbling driveway meets the country lane that winds up from the old A20 through Newington and Peene and then up the hill made by the Downs, to our gate.

A Gurkha lady had obviously been walking. They often take what for them is probably a short stroll from Folkestone up into the Downs. In reality, it's a walk that would probably put most of us into cardiac arrest. Without the campaign that lady wouldn't have been there. For some reason, this tiny flash of glimmering sari touched me profoundly. The feelings of the campaign and all that went with it swirled through my mind. It felt wonderful. It felt entirely right.

ACKNOWLEDGEMENTS

—————◆—————

The Gurkha Justice campaign was like a storm. It started slowly out of the limelight. It gathered strength over the ensuing months and years before finally building up to a mighty crescendo, bursting into the national consciousness. Along the way, it swept in a whole variety of people. Some made major contributions of money, others gave ideas. Some gave practical help. Some stayed with the campaign to the end; others helped build it for a while and then drifted away. Some were involved because it was their job to be, such as many of the journalists who reported on this remarkable story; others stepped forward because they felt that they wanted to help. Every contribution, however large or small, whether it was made over a few days or over many months, had its own unique place in, and value to, the campaign.

To describe every such person and their contribution would be a mammoth task – like describing a mosaic by detailing every individual piece.

The campaign started when I was an aspiring local Liberal Democrat politician. I think of my colleagues in Folkestone & Hythe Liberal Democrats: Miranda Roberts, Season Prater, Shaun Roberts, Tim Prater, Darren Briddock, Tessa Caruana, Troy Scaum, Sam Matthews, Neil Matthews, Matt Raines, Maggie Barrett-Sheldrake. Then there were the senior figures in the party over the years: Charles Kennedy, Ming Campbell, Nick Clegg and their respective staff members.

Numerous MPs played a part – principal among them, Bob Russell MP. Ann Widdecombe had been a champion of Gurkha affairs prior to the campaign and though she was not formally part of our campaigning work, her contribution to the welfare of Gurkhas should be marked.

Many friends have made their mark: Jo Underwood and Howard Cox spring to mind, to name but two.

Members of the public emerged as Gurkha champions in their own communities. I think particularly of 'Ray from Northampton', just one of many who took the signature gathering to their local high streets.

And of the many journalists involved, James Slack – then of the *Daily Express* – who gave us our major first break; Martyn Brown, also of the *Daily Express*; and Graham Brough of the *Daily Mirror*.